Betty Crocker's
125 Low-Calorie
Main Dishes

Prentice Hall

New York   London   Toronto   Sydney   Tokyo   Singapore

PRENTICE HALL GENERAL REFERENCE
15 Columbus Circle
New York, NY 10023

Copyright © 1992 by General Mills, Inc., Minneapolis, Minnesota

PRENTICE HALL and colophon are registered trademarks
of Simon & Schuster Inc.

BETTY CROCKER is a registered trademark of General Mills, Inc.

Library of Congress Cataloging-in-Publication Data

Crocker, Betty.
    [125 low-calorie main dishes]
    Betty Crocker's 125 low-calorie main dishes.
       p.   cm.
    Includes index.
    ISBN 0-13-085531-6
    1. Entrées (Cookery)   I. Title.
TX740.C688 1992
641.8′2—dc20   91-33759
                                               CIP

Designed by Frederick J. Latasa
Manufactured in the United States of America

10 9 8 7 6 5 4 3 2

First Edition

Contents

INTRODUCTION

Many of us want to lose weight at some point, and maintaining an appropriate weight is a goal shared by us all. With *Betty Crocker's 125 Low-Calorie Main Dishes*, you'll see that low-calorie dinners can have zest, flavor, diversity and be completely satisfying. Sample Beef Stroganoff, Chicken with Black Beans, Scampi with Fettuccini, Chicken and Tortellini Salad or Three Cheese Pie, and you'll be convinced that dieting can be delicious!

You'll also find nutrition information that will help you create a lifelong, healthful eating plan, from the explanation of a calorie to discussions of fat, cholesterol and sodium. We have also included our New Good-Eating Guide to help you choose appropriate foods. By following this easy guide, you'll learn how to eat properly balanced meals, as well as how to fit in foods you thought you'd have to give up forever, such as fried chicken, chocolate desserts and creamy sauces.

Throughout *Betty Crocker's 125 Low-Calorie Main Dishes* we have included additional tips and suggestions for weight loss and proper weight maintenance. You'll learn how to reduce calories in your own tried-and-true recipes, make your own cholesterol-wise egg substitute and much more.

Betty Crocker's 125 Low-Calorie Main Dishes will not only help you lose and maintain weight but make the experience pleasurable, healthful and surprisingly manageable!

THE BETTY CROCKER EDITORS

CHAPTER 1

GREAT GUIDELINES FOR LOW-CALORIE COOKING

LOSING WEIGHT—and maintaining that weight loss—is a concern for many of us. Faced with the tempting choices at supermarkets and specialty food shops and the convenience of fast-food restaurants, sometimes it feels as if the deck is stacked against us. Yet delicious, healthful meals that fit in comfortably with low-calorie eating plans can be exciting, diverse and very satisfying.

All the main dish recipes here contain 350 calories or less per serving, and can be incorporated easily into a lifelong eating plan. You'll find the New Good-Eating Guide (pages 4–6) to be invaluable in planning a healthful diet, whether you wish to lose weight, maintain weight or just eat well!

What Is a Calorie?

A calorie measures energy, specifically the energy produced when food is broken down by the body. Different foods provide the key nutrients we need—protein, carbohydrate and fat—and supply the body with energy in the form of calories.

Of course, different types of food provide different calorie amounts. By weight, fat has more than twice as many calories (9 calories per gram) as carbohydrate or protein (each 4 calories per gram). When you eat more high-fat foods than low-fat foods, you consume a great many more calories, without increasing the nutritional benefits.

To maintain a certain weight, a person should eat roughly the same number of calories as he or she expends through daily activities. If you decrease your activity while eating the same number of calories it's easy to gain weight. The good news is that, conversely, if you eat the same amount of food and raise your activity level through regular exercise, weight loss is sure to follow.

When following a weight-loss program it's vital to monitor your diet, but don't forget that adding regular exercise is also a major boost to weight loss and a more healthful lifestyle. And when maintaining your weight, regular exercise allows you to eat more food, as well as providing a host of other benefits.

Tips for Low-Calorie Main Dish Cooking

▲ Nonstick cookware and nonstick cooking spray lessen the amounts of fat used in cooking. Buying a 10- to 12-inch skillet and one or two saucepans stocks your pantry nicely.

▲ Cooking methods that use less fat are best. Broil, bake, roast, grill, poach, steam, stew and microwave foods whenever possible. Panfry and stir-fry, too, but only use small amounts of unsaturated oils.

▲ Choose lean cuts of meat and trim off the fat. Leaner cuts are now widely available. Trim visible fat before cooking. Because leaner cuts cook more quickly, watch timing carefully.

▲ The higher the grade of meat, the more fat it contains. The order of fat marbling from greatest to least is "Prime," "Choice" and "Select." When buying ground beef, choose extra lean.

▲ Remove the fat from cooking juices of meats, soups and stews by refrigerating or using a fat separator, then removing congealed fat.

▲ Reduce pan juices to your desired consistency and concentration of flavor when cooking meats, instead of making heavy sauces and gravies. This is most easily and quickly done by boiling skimmed juices in a skillet (liquid evaporates more quickly from a pan with a large surface area).

▲ Baste meats with their own juices, broth, fruit or vegetable juices rather than with margarine or butter.

▲ Limit added fats and oils to five to eight teaspoons a day. This amount includes such spreads as margarine, butter, mayonnaise and salad dressings. Try reduced-fat versions of these products.

▲ Serve such light meats as chicken, turkey or fish often. Light-meat poultry is naturally low in fat, especially if the skin is removed, and most fish is also very lean (see Fish, page 11).

▲ Skinned poultry can dry out easily when baked or roasted. Prepare with sauces or cover tightly when cooking. (See Chicken with Peppers and Onions, page 42.)

▲ Choose water-packed canned fish products, such as tuna, to limit your fat intake.

▲ Some dishes traditionally made with several eggs can be made successfully with only one or two whole eggs plus several egg whites. An example of this technique is Vegetable-filled Soufflé Roll (page 105).

▲ Use less cheese than usual, or choose low-fat cheese.

▲ Legumes, canned and dried, are low in fat and a high fiber protein source. Lentils are especially convenient as they have a short cooking time.

▲ Substitute complex carbohydrates for foods higher in fat, for example, a toasted whole wheat bagel for a cheese Danish. Complex carbohydrate is another term for starch and fiber; pasta, cereals, rice and potatoes are low-fat energy sources. Breads, vegetables and fruits are other excellent sources of complex carbohydrates.

▲ Serve more vegetables and fruits. When in season they are least expensive and best in flavor.

▲ Use low-fat, nonfat or skim milk products when cooking. There are many new milk products available, including cheeses and yogurts.

▲ Use strongly flavored ingredients in salad dressings and reduce or omit the amount of oil used.

Nutrition for the Nineties

In recent years, our major nutritional concerns have changed from nutrient deficiencies to the problem of having too much food. Health experts say that most people are eating too many calories and too much fat, saturated fat and cholesterol. Some of us are eating more sodium than is recommended. Instead of getting so many calories from fat, we should be getting the bulk of our calories from eating more carbohydrates, especially complex carbohydrates and fiber.

As scientists continue to explore the link between nutrition and health, we learn more about how to improve our health through better eating. The American diet has been associated with five leading causes of illness and death: coronary heart disease, certain types of cancer, stroke, diabetes mellitus and atherosclerosis. Health experts tell us that improving our diets may have a positive effect on the prevention and severity of these diseases.

The New Good-Eating Guide presents recommendations for vitamins and minerals as well as concerns about calories, carbohydrates, fiber, fat and cholesterol. Choose the recommended number of servings from the food groups listed to ensure adequate levels of these nutrients. Foods from "Eat Anytime" and "Eat in Moderation" categories will help you develop an eating plan that reflects recent nutritional concerns about calories and the sources of calories.

How to Use the New Good-Eating Guide

The New Good-Eating Guide (pages 4–6) combines the recommendations of health experts within an easy-to-use chart. It defines the same basic food groups as the original Good-Eating Guide, but separates items within each food group to help you make the best choice for a balanced diet.

A daily diet that includes the recommended number of servings from each group contains 1200 to 1800 calories. For those who require more calories, add more servings from the four groups and the "Others" category. If you're trying to cut calories, select foods in the "Eat Anytime" category more often than those in other categories.

The number of recommended servings per day from the four food groups has changed from the first version developed by nutritionists at the U.S. Department of Agriculture. Experts now recommend eating more foods from the bread and cereals group and the fruit and vegetable group. These foods are low in fat, high in carbohydrates and often provide complex carbohydrates and fiber as well.

Many foods we eat are combinations from more than one of the food groups. For example, a casserole with meat, pasta, vegetables and cheese contains ingredients from all four groups. To apply the New Good-Eating Guide to mixed dishes, be sure the dish has more ingredients from the "Eat Anytime" and "Eat in Moderation" groups than the "Eat Occasionally" group.

THE NEW GOOD-EATING GUIDE

	BREADS/CEREALS	FRUITS/VEGETABLES
	(6 to 11 servings daily. Includes whole grain, enriched breads and cereals, pasta, rice and crackers.)	(5 to 9 servings daily. Include at least one serving citrus or other choice high in vitamin C daily. Include orange or leafy, dark green vegetables 3 to 4 times a week.)
Recommended Serving Size	1 to 1.5 ounces ready-to-eat cereal (varies if it contains fruits, nuts) ½ cup cooked cereal, pasta or rice 1 slice bread ½ hamburger or hot dog bun ½ English muffin or bagel 1 small roll or muffin ½ pita (6 inches in diameter) 3 to 4 small or 2 large crackers 2 breadsticks (4 × ½ inch) 1 tortilla (6 inches in diameter) 3 cups popcorn 2 medium cookies	1 medium fruit such as apple, orange, banana ½ grapefruit ¾ cup juice 1 medium wedge melon ½ cup berries ¼ cup dried fruit ½ cup cooked or canned fruit or vegetable 1 medium potato 10 French-fried potatoes (2 to 3½ inches long) ½ cup raw chopped vegetables 1 cup leafy raw vegetable, such as spinach ⅛ medium avocado
Eat Anytime	Whole grain* or fortified breakfast cereal Whole grain* or enriched bread, rolls, bagels, English muffins, tortillas, low-fat crackers Brown or enriched white rice Whole grain or enriched pasta Plain popcorn, pretzels and low-fat cookies (such as fig bars) and cake (angel food)	All fresh, canned or frozen fruits and fruit juices All fresh, canned or frozen vegetables and vegetable juices Plain potato or potato with low-fat topping (such as yogurt)
Eat in Moderation	Biscuits Bread stuffing Corn bread Muffins and other quick breads Pancakes, waffles Popcorn made with added fat Taco shells	Vegetables with added butter or margarine Potatoes topped with butter, sour cream or sauces
Eat Occasionally	High-fat crackers Croissants Doughnuts Sweet rolls Snack chips (potato chips, corn chips, etc.) Most cookies and cakes	Fruit pies Deep-fried vegetables French-fried potatoes Vegetables in cream or cheese sauce
Key Nutrients Supplied	Complex carbohydrates Thiamin Iron Niacin Fiber	Vitamin A Vitamin C Fiber

*Good source of fiber.

**For those who need to limit sodium intake, these foods may be high in sodium (read nutrition labels for sodium content).

	MEAT/PROTEIN	MILK/DAIRY
	(2 to 3 servings with a total of about 6 ounces daily. Includes meat, fish, poultry and eggs. Dried beans, peas and nuts are alternatives.)	(2 servings daily: 3 for pregnant or breast-feeding women, 4 for pregnant or breast-feeding teenagers. Includes milk, yogurt, cheese, cottage cheese and pudding.)
Recommended Serving Size	2 ounces beef (maximum 3 ounces of beef daily) 2 ounces poultry or fish 4 ounces tofu Count the following as 1 ounce of meat: 　1 egg (maximum 3 eggs weekly) 　3 egg whites 　2 tablespoons peanut butter or whole nuts or seeds 　½ cup cooked beans, peas or lentils	1 cup milk 1 cup yogurt 1½ ounces cheese 1 cup pudding 1½ cups ice cream, ice milk or frozen yogurt 2 cups cottage cheese
Eat Anytime	*Beef:* Lean beef including round, sirloin, chuck and loin *Pork:* Lean cuts including ham and tenderloin *Lamb:* Leg, arm, loin, rib *Veal:* All trimmed cuts except ground *Poultry:* All poultry without skin *Fish:* All fresh and frozen fin fish or shellfish *Other:* Egg whites, all beans, peas and lentils	Skim milk 1% low-fat milk Low-fat buttermilk** Plain nonfat or low-fat yogurt Low-fat cheeses
Eat in Moderation	*Beef:* Most cuts including all ground beef, short ribs, corned beef brisket *Pork:* Most cuts including chops, loin roast *Poultry:* All poultry with skin *Other:* Fat-free or low-fat luncheon meats,** peanut butter and other nuts or seeds *Eggs:* Limit to three eggs per week	2% low-fat milk Part-skim milk cheese** Ice milk
Eat Occasionally	*Beef:* USDA prime-grade cuts and heavily marbled cuts *Pork:* Spareribs, ground pork *Lamb:* Ground lamb *Fish:* Fried fish *Other:* Luncheon meats**, sausage**, frankfurters**, bacon**	Whole milk, cream, half-and-half Whole milk yogurt All regular cheese** such as American, Cheddar, Brie, etc. Ice cream Cream cheese and sour cream
Key Nutrients	Protein Niacin Iron Thiamin	Calcium Riboflavin Protein

*Good source of fiber.

**For those who need to limit sodium intake, these foods may be high in sodium (read nutrition labels for sodium content).

The New Good-Eating Guide (*cont.*)

OTHERS

These foods supply energy (calories) and flavor, but are not good sources of key nutrients. Foods from the "Others" group should not replace those in the four food groups but can be used to enhance one's diet as recommended in the New Good-Eating Guide. Because these foods don't provide key nutrients, there are no recommended serving sizes. Apply balance and moderation when selecting these foods and the amounts eaten.

Fats and Oils

Butter
Cream and cream sauce
Gravy
Lard
Margarine
Mayonnaise
Oil
Salad dressing
Shortening

Condiments**

Barbecue sauce
Horseradish
Ketchup

Mustard
Olives
Pickles
Salt
Soy sauce
Taco sauce

Sweets

Candy
Honey
Jellies and jams
Sugar
Syrup

Alcohol

Beer
Hard liquor
Wine

Other Beverages

Coffee
Fruit drinks
Soft drinks
Tea

---

*Good source of fiber.
**For those who need to limit sodium intake, these foods may be high in sodium (read nutrition labels for sodium content).

Nutrition Information for Recipes

Each recipe in this book includes nutrition information per serving for calories, protein, carbohydrate, fat (and calories from fat), cholesterol and sodium. You'll find this information before each recipe.

▲ If ingredient choices are given, the first ingredient in the ingredient list was used to calculate the nutrition information.

▲ When a range is given for an ingredient, the first amount listed was used for nutrition calculation.

▲ Ingredients referred to as "if desired" are not included in the nutrition calculations, whether mentioned in the ingredient listing or in the recipe text as a suggestion.

▲ To be sure of the calories consumed, follow the serving sizes given in the recipes. Remember, if you eat more, you'll increase the calorie count.

Making Food Choices with the New Good-Eating Guide

To help you make smart choices within the food groups, the New Good-Eating Guide uses these categories:

Eat Anytime foods are low in calories, fat, saturated fat, cholesterol and, in many cases, sodium. They also may include significant amounts of complex carbohydrates and fiber. They're among the best choices to supply key nutrients from their respective food groups.

Eat in Moderation foods are also good sources of key nutrients but contain more fat and, in some cases, more saturated fat and cholesterol. But by controlling portion sizes and how often they are eaten, you can include these foods in a healthful diet.

Eat Occasionally foods are high in fat. While they aren't forbidden in a healthful diet, be certain to place even greater limits on portion size and how often these foods are eaten.

Healthful Eating with the New Good-Eating Guide

The concepts of variety, moderation and balance are basic to good nutrition and are flexible enough to suit individual tastes.

VARIETY is essential to ensure we're getting the nutrients we need for good health, and also makes eating nutritious foods more interesting. There's flexibility with the New Good-Eating Guide for making new choices without shortchanging old favorites. Long-term changes in diet can be easier through an approach that combines the old with the new.

MODERATION means limiting total calorie intake and foods high in fat, saturated fat and cholesterol, and for some people, it means limiting sodium. The New Good-Eating Guide makes moderation easy by recommending numbers of servings, portion sizes and the wisest choices within each food group. All foods are included in this guide because even foods high in fat, saturated fat and cholesterol can fit into a balanced diet—if they're eaten in moderation!

BALANCE means putting together a nutritious diet over a period of time. Although it's not desirable to make a whole meal out of "Eat Occasionally" foods, sometimes it happens. But by making smart choices for the next several meals, a healthful diet is still possible. The wisest choice is to balance those once-in-a-while choices with "Eat Anytime" foods.

Balance, variety and moderation apply to a lifestyle approach as well. Maintaining your ideal body weight, stopping smoking and doing regular exercise can add up to a more healthful you.

CHAPTER 2
SLIMMING SKILLET SPECIALTIES

Harvest Pork Tenderloins (page 31)

SALSA FISH

Cilantro, a southwestern favorite, is also known as fresh coriander, Mexican parsley and Chinese parsley. While cilantro resembles flat-leaf parsley, its flavor is more intense.

Per Serving			
Calories	150	Fat	2 g (18 calories)
Protein	24 g	Cholesterol	40 mg
Carbohydrate	6 g	Sodium	210 mg

4 Servings

1 pound cod, orange roughy or other medium-fat fish fillets (about ½ inch thick)

1 cup chopped tomato (about 1 large)

½ cup chopped green bell pepper (about 1 small)

¼ cup chopped onion (about 1 small)

2 tablespoons finely chopped fresh cilantro or parsley

¼ teaspoon salt

¼ cup dry white wine or chicken broth

If fish fillets are large, cut into 4 serving pieces. Spray 10-inch nonstick skillet with nonstick cooking spray. Heat over medium heat. Arrange fish in single layer in skillet. Cook uncovered 4 to 6 minutes, turning once, until fish flakes easily with fork. Remove fish to warm platter; keep warm.

Cook remaining ingredients except wine in skillet over medium heat 3 to 5 minutes, stirring frequently, until bell pepper and onion are crisp-tender. Stir in wine. Heat until hot. Spoon tomato mixture over fish.

ORANGE ROUGHY WITH RED PEPPERS

Per Serving			
Calories	145	Fat	3 g (27 calories)
Protein	23 g	Cholesterol	100 mg
Carbohydrate	7 g	Sodium	60 mg

4 Servings

1 pound orange roughy or other lean fish fillets

1 teaspoon olive or vegetable oil

1 small onion, cut into thin slices

2 red or green bell peppers, cut into julienne strips

1 tablespoon chopped fresh or 1 teaspoon dried thyme leaves

¼ teaspoon pepper

If fish fillets are large, cut into 4 serving pieces. Heat oil in 10-inch nonstick skillet. Layer onion and bell peppers in skillet; sprinkle with half of the thyme and pepper. Layer fish over bell peppers; sprinkle with remaining thyme and pepper.

Cover and cook over low heat 15 minutes. Uncover and cook 10 to 15 minutes longer or until fish flakes easily with fork.

If YOU LIKE FISH, you'll be interested to learn there are three classifications: lean, medium-fat and fatty. Fish is naturally rich in high-quality protein, yet low in fat, saturated fat, cholesterol and calories (see Counting Calories, pages 144–148). Percentages of fat in individual fish vary with the season, stage of maturity, locale, species and diet. One type of fish can be substituted for another of the same classification when preparing recipes.

Lean Fish contain less than 2.5 percent fat and are mild flavored with tender, white or pale flesh. Lean fish are best steamed, poached, microwaved or fried. Examples: Bass (sea or striped), burbot (freshwater cod), cod, cusk, flounder, grouper, haddock, halibut, lingcod, mackerel (king), mahimahi (dolphinfish), monkfish, orange roughy, perch (ocean), pike (northern), pollock, red snapper, rockfish, scrod, smelt, sole, tilefish, tuna (skipjack and yellowfin) and whiting.

Medium-Fat Fish with 2.5 to 5 percent fat content are suitable for all cooking methods. Examples: Anchovy, bluefish, catfish, croaker, mullet, porgy, redfish, salmon (pink), shark, swordfish, trout (rainbow and sea), tuna (bluefin), turbot and whitefish.

Fatty Fish have a fat content greater than 5 percent, and generally have a firmer texture, more pronounced flavor and a deeper color. Fatty fish are best broiled, grilled, baked or microwaved. Examples: Butterfish, carp, eel, herring, mackerel (Atlantic, Pacific and Spanish), pompano, sablefish, salmon (chinook, coho and sockeye), sardines, shad and trout (lake).

SHRIMP WITH FETA CHEESE

Per Serving			
Calories	340	Fat 14 g (126 calories)	
Protein	23 g	Cholesterol	295 mg
Carbohydrate	28 g	Sodium	1040 mg

4 Servings, about 1¼ cups each

1 pound fresh or frozen raw medium shrimp (in shells)

1 cup chopped onion (about 1 large)

2 cloves garlic, chopped

3 tablespoons olive or vegetable oil

½ cup dry white wine

1 tablespoon chopped fresh or 1 teaspoon dried basil leaves

1 tablespoon chopped fresh or 1 teaspoon dried oregano leaves

Dash of ground red pepper (cayenne)

1 can (28 ounces) Italian pear-shaped tomatoes, drained and chopped

2 tablespoons lemon juice

2 ounces feta cheese, crumbled

Chopped fresh parsley

Peel shrimp. (If shrimp are frozen, do not thaw; peel in cold water.) Make a shallow cut lengthwise down back of each shrimp; wash out vein. Cook onion and garlic in oil in 10-inch skillet over medium heat, stirring occasionally, until onion is softened.

Stir in wine, basil, oregano, red pepper and tomatoes. Heat to boiling; reduce heat. Simmer uncovered 20 minutes. Stir in shrimp and lemon juice. Cover and cook 3 to 5 minutes or until shrimp are pink. Sprinkle with cheese and parsley. Serve with hot cooked rice if desired.

HALIBUT STIR-FRY

Sesame oil with its high smoking point is perfect for a stir-fry. We suggest using darker, Oriental sesame oil in this recipe as it has a more robust flavor than light sesame oil.

Per Serving			
Calories	195	Fat 5 g (45 calories)	
Protein	27 g	Cholesterol	35 mg
Carbohydrate	10 g	Sodium	730 mg

4 Servings, about 2 cups each

2 teaspoons sesame oil

1 pound halibut or other lean fish steaks, cut into 1-inch pieces

1 medium onion, thinly sliced

3 cloves garlic, finely chopped

1 teaspoon finely chopped gingerroot

1 package (10 ounces) frozen asparagus cuts, thawed and drained

1 cup sliced mushrooms (about 3 ounces) or 1 can (4 ounces) sliced mushrooms, drained

1 medium tomato, cut into thin wedges

2 tablespoons soy sauce

1 tablespoon lemon juice

Heat oil in 10-inch nonstick skillet over medium-high heat. Add fish, onion, garlic, gingerroot and asparagus; stir-fry 2 to 3 minutes or until fish almost flakes with fork. Carefully stir in remaining ingredients; heat thoroughly. Serve with additional soy sauce if desired.

Shrimp with Feta Cheese

Stir-fried Shrimp with Vegetables

A stir-fry cooks in a flash, so be sure to have all your ingredients chopped and ready before you begin cooking.

	Per Serving		
Calories	205	Fat	10 g (90 calories)
Protein	17 g	Cholesterol	195 mg
Carbohydrate	12 g	Sodium	1030 mg

4 Servings, about 1½ cups each

1 pound fresh or frozen raw medium shrimp (in shells)

1 teaspoon cornstarch

½ teaspoon salt

½ teaspoon sesame oil

⅛ teaspoon white pepper

7 large stalks bok choy

6 ounces Chinese pea pods

2 green onions with tops, cut into 2-inch pieces

2 tablespoons oyster sauce or 1 tablespoon dark soy sauce

1 tablespoon cornstarch

1 tablespoon cold water

2 tablespoons vegetable oil

1 teaspoon finely chopped gingerroot

1 teaspoon finely chopped garlic

1 tablespoon vegetable oil

1½ cups (about 4 ounces) ½-inch slices mushrooms

½ teaspoon salt

½ cup chicken broth

Peel shrimp. (If shrimp are frozen, do not thaw; peel in cold water.) Make a shallow cut lengthwise down back of each shrimp; wash out vein. Pat dry with paper towels. Toss shrimp, 1 teaspoon cornstarch, ½ teaspoon salt, the sesame oil and white pepper in medium bowl. Cover and refrigerate 20 minutes.

Remove leaves from bok choy stems. Cut leaves into 2-inch pieces. Cut stems diagonally into ¼-inch slices (do not combine leaves and stems). Remove strings from pea pods. Place pea pods in boiling water. Cover and cook 1 minute; drain. Immediately rinse with cold water; drain.

Shred onion pieces lengthwise into fine strips. Cover with iced water; let stand 10 minutes or until strips are curled. Mix oyster sauce, 1 tablespoon cornstarch and 1 tablespoon cold water.

Heat wok or 12-inch skillet until very hot. Add 2 tablespoons vegetable oil; rotate wok to coat sides. Add shrimp, gingerroot and garlic; stir-fry until shrimp are pink. Remove from wok.

Heat wok until very hot. Add 1 tablespoon vegetable oil; rotate wok to coat side. Add bok choy stems, mushrooms and ½ teaspoon salt; stir-fry 1 minute. Add bok choy leaves and broth; heat to boiling. Stir in cornstarch mixture; cook and stir until thickened. Add shrimp and pea pods; cook and stir 1 minute or until shrimp are hot. Garnish with onions.

SCALLOPS IN WINE SAUCE

Per Serving			
Calories	330	Fat 14 g (126 calories)	
Protein	28 g	Cholesterol	60 mg
Carbohydrate	10 g	Sodium	380 mg

4 Servings, about 1½ cups each

- **1½ cups sliced mushrooms (about 4 ounces)**
- **⅓ cup sliced leek with green top (about 1 small)**
- **2 tablespoons reduced-calorie margarine**
- **2 tablespoons olive or vegetable oil**
- **½ cup dry white wine**
- **½ teaspoon chopped fresh or ⅛ teaspoon dried tarragon leaves**
- **1 pound bay scallops**
- **2 teaspoons cornstarch**
- **2 tablespoons cold water**
- **3 cups shredded lettuce**
- **1 lemon, cut into wedges**

Cook mushrooms and leek in margarine and oil in 10-inch skillet 5 minutes, stirring occasionally. Stir in wine and tarragon. Heat to boiling. Stir in scallops; reduce heat. Cook uncovered 3 to 4 minutes, stirring occasionally, until scallops are white.

Mix cornstarch and water; stir into scallop mixture. Heat to boiling, stirring constantly. Boil and stir 1 minute. Spoon scallop mixture over lettuce; garnish with lemon.

SCALLOPS WITH VEGETABLES

Can't find bay scallops? Use sea scallops and cut them in halves or quarters so they are approximately ½ inch in diameter, so the same cooking time can be used.

Per Serving			
Calories	160	Fat 2 g (18 calories)	
Protein	28 g	Cholesterol	60 mg
Carbohydrate	12 g	Sodium	460 mg

4 Servings, about ¾ cup each

- **1 pound bay scallops**
- **¼ cup sliced green onions with tops (about 2 medium)**
- **¼ teaspoon salt**
- **⅛ teaspoon white pepper**
- **1 clove garlic, finely chopped**
- **1 package (9 ounces) frozen artichoke hearts, thawed and drained, or 1 can (14 ounces) artichoke hearts, drained and cut into fourths**
- **1 cup cherry tomatoes (about 10), cut into fourths**
- **1 cup shredded romaine or spinach**
- **1 tablespoon lemon juice**

Cook scallops, onions, salt, pepper and garlic in 10-inch nonstick skillet over medium-high heat 4 minutes, stirring frequently. Stir in artichoke hearts. Cook 3 to 4 minutes or until scallops are white. Stir in tomatoes and romaine. Cook until tomatoes are hot and romaine is wilted, stirring occasionally; drain. Sprinkle with lemon juice.

DILLED LEMON CHICKEN

Per Serving			
Calories	350	Fat 12 g (108 calories)	
Protein	25 g	Cholesterol	95 mg
Carbohydrate	30 g	Sodium	210 mg

6 Servings

1 tablespoon reduced-calorie margarine

6 skinless boneless chicken breast halves (about 1½ pounds)

½ cup dry white wine or chicken broth

1 tablespoon lemon juice

¼ teaspoon salt

1 teaspoon chopped fresh or ⅛ teaspoon dried dill weed

½ lemon, thinly sliced

¼ cup sliced green onions with tops (about 2 medium)

3 cups hot cooked rice

Heat margarine in 10-inch nonstick skillet over medium heat. Cook chicken breast halves in margarine about 10 minutes, turning once, until light brown. Mix wine, lemon juice, salt and dill weed; pour over chicken. Place lemon slices on chicken.

Heat to boiling; reduce heat. Cover and simmer 10 to 15 minutes or until juices of chicken run clear. Remove chicken; keep warm. Heat wine mixture to boiling; boil about 3 minutes or until reduced to about half. Pour over chicken. Sprinkle with onions, and serve with rice.

CHICKEN WITH RED PEPPERS

Per Serving			
Calories	350	Fat 15 g (135 calories)	
Protein	45 g	Cholesterol	135 mg
Carbohydrate	8 g	Sodium	370 mg

6 Servings

1 tablespoon olive or vegetable oil

3 to 3½ pounds broiler-fryer chicken pieces

½ cup chopped onion (about 1 medium)

1 clove garlic, chopped

3 red bell peppers, cut into thin strips

1½ cups chopped tomatoes (about 2 medium)

¼ cup chopped prosciutto (about 1 ounce)

½ teaspoon salt

¼ teaspoon pepper

3 cups hot cooked spaghetti or linguine

Heat oil in 12-inch nonstick skillet. Cook chicken over medium heat about 15 minutes or until brown on all sides. Remove chicken. Cook onion and garlic in oil, stirring occasionally, until onion is softened. Stir in remaining ingredients except spaghetti. Heat to boiling; reduce heat.

Return chicken to skillet. Simmer uncovered about 40 minutes, turning chicken pieces occasionally, until juices of thickest pieces of chicken run clear. Remove chicken to warm platter; keep warm. Cook sauce over medium heat about 5 minutes, stirring occasionally, until very thick. Serve sauce over chicken and spaghetti.

Chicken with Red Peppers

Scandinavian Chicken with Apricots

For a delicious difference, substitute dried apples and apple brandy for the apricots and apricot brandy.

Per Serving

Calories	250	Fat	4 g (18 calories)
Protein	28 g	Cholesterol	70 mg
Carbohydrate	18 g	Sodium	260 mg

6 Servings

½ cup water

¼ cup apricot brandy

1 package (6 ounces) dried apricots (about 1¼ cups)

2 tablespoons currants

1 tablespoon vegetable oil

6 skinless boneless chicken breast halves (about 1½ pounds)

½ teaspoon salt

2 teaspoons chopped fresh or ½ teaspoon dried thyme leaves

¼ teaspoon pepper

1 lemon, thinly sliced

⅓ cup slivered almonds, toasted (if desired)

Mix water, brandy, apricots and currants; let stand 15 minutes.

Heat oil in 12-inch nonstick skillet. Cook chicken over medium heat about 15 minutes or until brown on all sides; drain fat. Sprinkle chicken with salt, thyme and pepper. Add apricot mixture and lemon slices. Heat to boiling; reduce heat. Cover and simmer 35 to 40 minutes, spooning pan juices over chicken occasionally, until juices of chicken run clear. Sprinkle with almonds.

SPICY CHICKEN WITH BROCCOLI

Brown bean sauce, or paste, is a thick, savory sauce made from fermented yellow soybeans, flour and salt. You'll find it in the international-foods section of your supermarket. If it's not available, you can substitute the same amount of dark soy sauce.

Per Serving			
Calories	305	Fat 13 g (117 calories)	
Protein	37 g	Cholesterol	85 mg
Carbohydrate	10 g	Sodium	420 mg

4 Servings, about 1½ cups each

2 whole chicken breasts (about 2 pounds)

2 teaspoons cornstarch

½ teaspoon salt

¼ teaspoon white pepper

1 pound broccoli

3 green onions with tops

1 jalapeño chili or 1 teaspoon dried red pepper flakes

3 tablespoons vegetable oil

2 tablespoons brown bean sauce

2 teaspoons finely chopped garlic

1 teaspoon sugar

1 teaspoon finely chopped gingerroot

Remove bones and skin from chicken breasts; cut chicken into 2 × ½-inch pieces. Toss chicken, cornstarch, salt and white pepper in medium bowl. Cover and refrigerate 20 minutes.

Pare outer layer from broccoli. Cut broccoli lengthwise into 1-inch stems; remove flowerets. Cut stems diagonally into ¼-inch slices. Place broccoli flowerets and stems in boiling water; heat to boiling. Cover and cook 1 minute; drain. Immediately rinse with cold water; drain. Cut onions diagonally into 1-inch pieces. Remove seeds and membrane from chili. Cut chili into very thin slices.

Heat wok or 12-inch skillet until very hot. Add 3 tablespoons oil; rotate wok to coat side. Add chili, bean sauce, garlic, sugar and gingerroot; stir-fry 10 seconds. Add chicken; stir-fry 2 minutes or until chicken is white. Add broccoli and onions; stir-fry 1 minute or until broccoli is hot.

CHICKEN RATATOUILLE

Sprinkle lightly with freshly grated Parmesan cheese for extra flavor at only a few calories!

─── Per Serving ───			
Calories	350	Fat 13 g (117 calories)	
Protein	43 g	Cholesterol	125 mg
Carbohydrate	12 g	Sodium	490 mg

6 Servings

- **1 tablespoon all-purpose flour**
- **½ teaspoon salt**
- **1 teaspoon paprika**
- **⅛ teaspoon pepper**
- **3 to 3½ pounds broiler-fryer chicken pieces**
- **1 tablespoon vegetable oil**
- **¼ cup water**
- **3 cloves garlic, finely chopped**
- **1 tablespoon chopped fresh or 1 teaspoon dried basil leaves**
- **¼ teaspoon pepper**
- **4 cups 1-inch pieces eggplant (about 1 pound)**
- **2 cups sliced zucchini (about 2 small)**
- **1 medium green bell pepper, cut into 1-inch pieces**
- **½ cup chopped onion (about 1 medium)**
- **3 medium tomatoes, cut into wedges**
- **½ teaspoon salt**

Mix flour, ½ teaspoon salt, the paprika and ⅛ teaspoon pepper; sprinkle over chicken.

Heat oil in 12-inch nonstick skillet or 4-quart Dutch oven. Cook chicken over medium heat about 15 minutes or until brown on all sides; add water. Heat to boiling; reduce heat. Cover and simmer 20 minutes.

Mix garlic, basil and ¼ teaspoon pepper. Add eggplant to skillet; sprinkle with half of the garlic mixture. Add zucchini, bell pepper and onion; sprinkle with remaining garlic mixture. Add 1 to 2 tablespoons water if necessary. Cover and simmer 10 to 15 minutes, stirring occasionally, until juices of thickest pieces of chicken run clear and vegetables are crisp-tender. Add tomato wedges; sprinkle with ½ teaspoon salt. Cover and simmer about 5 minutes or until tomatoes are hot.

RASPBERRY-PEACH CHICKEN

Per Serving			
Calories	255	Fat	5 g (45 calories)
Protein	27 g	Cholesterol	19 mg
Carbohydrate	19 g	Sodium	210 mg

4 Servings

½ cup fresh or frozen raspberries

1 small peach, peeled and sliced

2 tablespoons peach brandy or apple juice

2 tablespoons honey

¼ cup all-purpose flour

¼ teaspoon salt

¼ teaspoon pepper

4 skinless boneless chicken breast halves (about 1 pound)

1 tablespoon vegetable oil

Place raspberries, peach slices, brandy and honey in blender or food processor. Cover and blend on high speed or process about 1 minute or until smooth. Heat in 1-quart saucepan over medium heat until hot, stirring occasionally. Keep warm.

Mix flour, salt and pepper. Coat chicken breast halves with flour mixture. Heat oil in 10-inch skillet. Cook chicken over medium heat 12 to 14 minutes, turning once, until juices of chicken run clear. Serve chicken with sauce. Garnish with additional raspberries, and serve with rice if desired.

CHICKEN WITH PINEAPPLE

Per Serving			
Calories	350	Fat 13 g (117 calories)	
Protein	42 g	Cholesterol	125 mg
Carbohydrate	14 g	Sodium	550 mg

6 Servings

1 tablespoon olive or vegetable oil

3 to 3½ pounds broiler-fryer chicken pieces

½ cup chopped onion (about 1 medium)

2 cloves garlic, chopped

1 pineapple, pared and cut into 1-inch pieces, or 1 can (20 ounces) unsweetened pineapple chunks, drained

½ cup chicken broth or dry sherry

2 tablespoons vinegar

1 teaspoon salt

¼ teaspoon ground cinnamon

¼ teaspoon ground cloves

⅛ teaspoon pepper

1½ cups coarsely chopped tomatoes (about 2 medium)

3 cups hot cooked rice

Heat oil in 12-inch nonstick skillet. Cook chicken over medium heat about 15 minutes or until brown on all sides. Remove chicken. Cook onion and garlic in oil, stirring occasionally, until onion is softened.

Return chicken to skillet. Mix remaining ingredients except tomatoes and rice; pour over chicken. Heat to boiling; reduce heat.

Cover and simmer 20 minutes. Add tomatoes; simmer uncovered about 20 minutes or until juices of thickest pieces of chicken run clear. Serve with rice.

TURKEY WITH APRICOT CHUTNEY

Per Serving			
Calories	265	Fat 12 g (108 calories)	
Protein	25 g	Cholesterol	75 mg
Carbohydrate	12 g	Sodium	220 mg

4 Servings, with about 3 tablespoons chutney each

1 tablespoon reduced-calorie margarine

1 tablespoon packed brown sugar

1 tablespoon lime juice

½ teaspoon grated gingerroot or ¼ teaspoon ground ginger

¼ teaspoon salt

⅛ teaspoon crushed red pepper

⅛ teaspoon ground cardamom

4 ripe apricots, peeled and coarsely chopped, or 1 can (8½ ounces) apricot halves in syrup, drained and coarsely chopped

2 tablespoons raisins

2 tablespoons water

2 teaspoons vegetable oil

1 pound turkey breast slices or cutlets (¼ to ½ inch thick)

Heat margarine, brown sugar, lime juice, gingerroot, salt, red pepper and cardamom in 1½-quart saucepan over medium heat 2 minutes. Stir in apricots, raisins and water; reduce heat to low. Cook, stirring occasionally, until liquid is evaporated; remove from heat. Cool slightly.

Heat 1 teaspoon oil in 10-inch nonstick skillet over medium-high heat. Sauté half of the turkey breast slices about 4 minutes, turning once, until no longer pink. Remove turkey from skillet; keep warm. Repeat with remaining 1 teaspoon oil and turkey breast slices. Serve apricot chutney over turkey.

Cold Poached Turkey with Curry Sauce

A great do-ahead recipe—add fresh sliced tomatoes for an easy lunch or dinner.

	Per Serving		
Calories	220	Fat	8 g (72 calories)
Protein	27 g	Cholesterol	75 mg
Carbohydrate	7 g	Sodium	300 mg

6 Servings, with about 3 tablespoons sauce each

- **2 turkey tenderloins (about 1½ pounds)**
- **2 tablespoons lemon juice**
- **2 teaspoons chicken bouillon granules**
- **⅛ teaspoon crushed red pepper**
- **1 small onion, cut into fourths**
- **1 clove garlic, cut in half**
- **Curry Sauce (right)**
- **Leaf lettuce**

Place all ingredients except Curry Sauce and lettuce in 4-quart Dutch oven. Add just enough water to cover turkey (2½ to 3 cups). Heat to boiling; reduce heat. Cover and simmer about 30 minutes or until turkey is done. Refrigerate turkey in broth until cool. Prepare Curry Sauce.

Line serving platter with leaf lettuce. Slice turkey diagonally across the grain into ¼-inch slices. Serve turkey with Curry Sauce. Garnish with tomato wedges and cilantro if desired.

Curry Sauce

- **1 cup plain nonfat yogurt**
- **1 tablespoon chutney, chopped**
- **2 teaspoons chopped fresh cilantro**
- **1 teaspoon curry powder**
- **Dash of ground red pepper (cayenne)**

Mix all ingredients. Cover and refrigerate.

Confetti Corned Beef Hash

	Per Serving		
Calories	270	Fat	17 g (153 calories)
Protein	15 g	Cholesterol	160 mg
Carbohydrate	12 g	Sodium	710 mg

4 Servings, about 1 cup each

- **2 tablespoons reduced-calorie margarine**
- **2 cups chopped cooked potatoes (about 2 medium)**
- **1½ cups cut-up cooked corned beef or lean cooked beef (about 8 ounces)**
- **½ cup chopped bell pepper (about 1 small)**
- **¼ cup sliced green onions with tops (about 2 medium)**
- **2 tablespoons chopped fresh parsley**
- **1 teaspoon chopped fresh or ¼ teaspoon dried thyme leaves**
- **2 hard-cooked eggs, chopped**

Heat margarine in 10-inch nonstick skillet over medium heat. Stir in remaining ingredients. Cook uncovered 8 to 10 minutes, turning frequently, until hot.

Beef Stroganoff

		Per Serving		
Calories	280	Fat	7 g (63 calories)	
Protein	26 g	Cholesterol	75 mg	
Carbohydrate	25 g	Sodium	460 mg	

6 Servings, about ⅔ cup beef mixture
and ½ cup noodles each

1-pound lean beef boneless round steak, about ½ inch thick

1 tablespoon reduced-calorie margarine

½ cup chopped onion (about 1 medium)

1 clove garlic, finely chopped

3 cups sliced mushrooms (about 8 ounces)

¼ cup dry red wine

2 tablespoons cornstarch

1 cup condensed beef broth

¼ teaspoon pepper

¾ cup plain nonfat yogurt

2 cups hot cooked noodles or rice

2 tablespoons chopped fresh parsley

Trim fat from beef steak; cut beef with grain into 2-inch strips. Cut strips diagonally across grain into ¼-inch slices. (For ease in cutting, partially freeze beef, about 1½ hours.) Heat margarine in 10-inch nonstick skillet over medium heat. Cook onion and garlic, stirring occasionally, until onion is softened. Stir in beef and mushrooms. Cook about 7 minutes, stirring occasionally, until beef is no longer pink. Stir in wine; reduce heat. Cover and simmer 10 minutes.

Mix cornstarch and broth; stir into beef mixture. Cook over medium-high heat, stirring occasionally, until thickened; remove from heat. Stir in pepper and yogurt; reduce heat. Cover and simmer about 30 minutes, stirring occasionally, until beef is tender. Serve over noodles; sprinkle with parsley.

ORIENTAL BEEF WITH RICE NOODLES

Chinese rice noodles are sold packaged in coiled nests, or as rice sticks, cut ¼ inch wide. They are also found cut extremely thin and fine.

——— Per Serving ———			
Calories	205	Fat	5 g (45 calories)
Protein	18 g	Cholesterol	40 mg
Carbohydrate	18 g	Sodium	380 mg

4 Servings, about 1¾ cups each

¾-pound lean beef boneless round steak

2 tablespoons sake (rice wine), sherry or chicken broth

1 tablespoon finely chopped ginger-root or 1 teaspoon ground ginger

2 teaspoons vegetable oil

½ teaspoon salt

1 clove garlic, crushed

4 ounces rice sticks

1 teaspoon vegetable oil

2 cups thinly sliced bok choy with leaves (about 3 large stalks)

½ cup sliced green onions with tops (about 4 medium)

1 can (15 ounces) straw mushrooms, drained*

2 tablespoons sake (rice wine), sherry or chicken broth

Trim fat from beef steak. Cut beef diagonally into ¼-inch strips. Mix beef, 2 tablespoons sake, the gingerroot, 2 teaspoons oil, the salt and garlic in medium glass or plastic bowl. Cover and refrigerate 30 minutes.

Place rice sticks in large bowl. Cover with hot water. Let stand 10 minutes; drain well. Chop coarsely.

Heat 1 teaspoon oil in wok or 12-inch skillet until very hot. Add beef mixture; stir-fry about 5 minutes or until beef is done. Add rice sticks, bok choy, onions and mushrooms; stir-fry about 4 minutes or until bok choy is crisp-tender. Sprinkle with 2 tablespoons sake.

*2 jars (4.5 ounces each) whole mushrooms, drained, can be substituted for the straw mushrooms.

Beef Medallions with Cucumber Relish

Per Serving			
Calories	170	Fat	8 g (72 calories)
Protein	20 g	Cholesterol	60 mg
Carbohydrate	3 g	Sodium	160 mg

6 Servings, with about 3 tablespoons relish each

Cucumber Relish (below)

1-pound lean beef tenderloin

1 tablespoon reduced-calorie margarine

1 clove garlic, finely chopped

Prepare Cucumber Relish. Cut beef crosswise into 6 slices. Pound slices to ½-inch thickness. Heat margarine in 10-inch nonstick skillet over medium-high heat. Sauté garlic about 1 minute or until garlic begins to brown. Add beef; sauté about 7 minutes, turning once, for medium doneness. Serve with Cucumber Relish.

Cucumber Relish

1 cup chopped seeded pared cucumber (about 1 medium)

¼ cup finely chopped onion (about 1 small)

¼ cup plain nonfat yogurt

1 tablespoon chopped fresh parsley

1 tablespoon chopped fresh or 1 teaspoon dried cilantro

1 tablespoon lemon juice

¼ teaspoon salt

1 clove garlic, finely chopped

Mix all ingredients; cover and let stand.

French-style Beef Roast

Per Serving			
Calories	265	Fat	8 g (72 calories)
Protein	36 g	Cholesterol	105 mg
Carbohydrate	9 g	Sodium	390 mg

8 Servings

3-pound beef boneless chuck or rolled rump roast

1 teaspoon salt

1 tablespoon chopped fresh or 1 teaspoon dried thyme leaves

1 bay leaf

1 large clove garlic, cut into fourths

6 whole cloves

5 peppercorns

4 cups water

4 medium carrots, cut crosswise in half

2 medium onions, cut into fourths

2 medium turnips, cut into fourths

2 medium stalks celery, cut into 1-inch pieces

Place beef roast, salt, thyme, bay leaf, garlic, cloves and peppercorns in 4-quart Dutch oven; add water. Heat to boiling; reduce heat. Cover and simmer 2½ hours.

Add remaining ingredients. Cover and simmer about 30 minutes or until beef and vegetables are tender. Remove beef; cut into ¼-inch slices. Serve vegetables with beef. Strain broth; serve with beef and vegetables.

If YOU LOVE MEAT, you probably noticed the new types of beef and pork sold in supermarkets. Since more consumers are concerned about fat and cholesterol, animals are now being bred to be leaner. And while in the past you may have seen up to ½ inch of fat covering a beef or pork cut, today those same cuts will only have ⅛ to ¼ inch of fat covering.

For the fewest calories per serving, trim all visible fat before cooking and use lean-cooking methods such as broiling, pan broiling, roasting, grilling or microwaving.

These leaner meats are more sensitive to cooking and especially to overcooking. Watch meats carefully and cook them just until tender or to the temperatures indicated. With less fat within the muscle tissue, even a few degrees over the specified temperature can overcook meats and cause them to toughen.

To avoid any food safety problems, ground beef should be cooked to at least medium doneness (160° or higher), while large beef cuts such as steaks and roasts can still be cooked to rare (140°) if desired.

New directions for cooking large pork cuts such as steaks and roasts now give you the option of cooking to 160° (which may be very slightly pink) or 170°, well-done, whichever you prefer. The lower temperatures allow the leaner meats to retain their juiciness and tenderness.

FIG AND ALMOND LAMB CHOPS

Per Serving			
Calories	300	Fat 9 g (81 calories)	
Protein	26 g	Cholesterol	85 mg
Carbohydrate	27 g	Sodium	200 mg

4 Servings, with about ¼ cup fruit each

4 lean lamb loin or rib chops (about 1 pound)

¼ cup water

¼ cup dry red wine or beef broth

2 tablespoons frozen orange juice concentrate, thawed

2 teaspoons chopped fresh or ½ teaspoon dried rosemary leaves

¼ teaspoon salt

1 clove garlic, finely chopped

½ cup dried figs, cut into halves

½ cup dried apricot halves

2 tablespoons slivered almonds, toasted

Remove fell (the paperlike covering) from lamb chops, if necessary; trim fat. Cook lamb in 10-inch nonstick skillet over medium heat until brown on both sides.

Mix water, wine, orange juice concentrate, rosemary, salt and garlic. Pour over lamb. Arrange figs and apricots around lamb. Cover and cook 10 minutes. Uncover and cook until lamb is done and liquid is almost evaporated and slightly thickened. Remove lamb and fruit to serving platter. Sprinkle with almonds.

CRANBERRY PORK CHOPS

Be careful not to overcook lean pork chops, or they will become tough.

Per Serving			
Calories	350	Fat 13 g (117 calories)	
Protein	25 g	Cholesterol	80 mg
Carbohydrate	33 g	Sodium	170 mg

4 Servings

4 lean pork loin chops, about ½ inch thick (about 1 pound)

2 teaspoons chopped fresh or ½ teaspoon dried sage

¼ teaspoon pepper

¼ cup chicken broth

2 medium turnips (about ½ pound), pared and cut into 2 × ½ × ½-inch strips

1 cup whole berry cranberry sauce

½ cup chopped onion (about 1 medium)

Trim fat from pork chops. Cook pork in 10-inch nonstick skillet over medium heat until brown on both sides. Sprinkle with sage and pepper. Pour broth around pork. Layer turnips around pork. Cover and simmer 15 minutes.

Mix cranberry sauce and onion; spoon onto pork. Cover and simmer about 15 minutes or until turnips are tender and pork is done.

HARVEST PORK TENDERLOINS

Per Serving			
Calories	215	Fat	6 g (54 calories)
Protein	20 g	Cholesterol	60 mg
Carbohydrate	21 g	Sodium	190 mg

4 Servings

¾-pound lean pork tenderloin, cut into 4 slices

2 teaspoons olive or vegetable oil

½ cup chopped onion (about 1 medium)

2 teaspoons chopped fresh or ½ teaspoon dried rosemary leaves, crushed

¼ teaspoon salt

⅛ teaspoon pepper

1 clove garlic, finely chopped

2 cups cubed acorn or butternut squash

1 cup chopped apple (about 1 medium)

2 tablespoons raisins

½ cup apple cider or apple juice

Pound pork tenderloin slices until ½ inch thick. Heat oil in 10-inch nonstick skillet over medium heat. Cook pork, turning once, about 12 minutes or until done. Remove pork from skillet; keep warm.

Cook onion, rosemary, salt, pepper and garlic in skillet over medium heat about 3 minutes, stirring occasionally, until onion is tender. Stir in remaining ingredients. Top with pork. Reduce heat to low. Cover and cook about 10 minutes or until squash is tender.

SKILLET PORK AND ONIONS

Per Serving			
Calories	350	Fat 13 g (117 calories)	
Protein	20 g	Cholesterol	65 mg
Carbohydrate	38 g	Sodium	510 mg

6 Servings, about 1½ cups each

1½ pounds pork boneless shoulder

1 tablespoon olive or vegetable oil

¼ cup water

3 medium onions, sliced

1 cup chopped tomato (about 1 large)

1 teaspoon salt

½ teaspoon paprika

¼ teaspoon pepper

¼ teaspoon crushed red pepper

1 green bell pepper, cut into strips

2 ounces feta cheese, cut into ¾-inch cubes

3 cups hot cooked rice

Trim fat from pork shoulder. Cut pork into ½-inch slices; cut slices into ½-inch strips. (For ease in cutting, partially freeze pork, about 1 hour.) Heat oil in 10-inch skillet. Cook pork over medium heat about 15 minutes, stirring occasionally, until brown; drain. Stir in water, onions, tomato, salt, paprika, pepper and red pepper. Cover and simmer about 30 minutes or until pork is tender. (Add water if necessary.)

Stir in bell pepper. Cover and simmer about 5 minutes or until bell pepper is crisp-tender. Top with cheese. Serve with rice.

Italian Sausage and Vegetables

Try cutting the spaghetti squash crosswise; you'll have longer strands than if you cut it lengthwise.

——————— Per Serving ———————			
Calories	275	Fat 16 g (144 calories)	
Protein	17 g	Cholesterol	45 mg
Carbohydrate	18 g	Sodium	790 mg

6 Servings, about 1¾ cups each

1 spaghetti squash (about 3 pounds)

1 pound Italian sausage, casing removed and sausage crumbled, or bulk Italian sausage

½ cup chopped onion (about 1 medium)

1 cup coarsely chopped zucchini (about 1 medium)

¼ cup chopped fresh parsley

1 large clove garlic, crushed

3 tablespoons chopped fresh or 1 tablespoon dried basil leaves

3 cups coarsely chopped tomatoes (about 3 large)

⅓ cup grated Parmesan cheese

½ teaspoon salt

¼ teaspoon pepper

Heat oven to 400°. Prick squash with fork. Bake about 1 hour or until tender.

Cook sausage and onion in 10-inch nonstick skillet over medium heat about 10 minutes, stirring occasionally, until sausage is done; drain. Stir in zucchini, parsley, garlic and basil. Cover and cook 3 minutes. Stir in tomatoes and cheese. Cut squash in half; remove seeds and fibers. Remove spaghetti-like strands, using 2 forks; toss with salt and pepper. Serve sausage mixture over squash.

HAM AND ZUCCHINI

You can substitute cooked smoked turkey for the ham if you like.

———————	Per Serving	———————	
Calories	270	Fat	7 g (63 calories)
Protein	22 g	Cholesterol	50 mg
Carbohydrate	29 g	Sodium	980 mg

6 Servings, about 1½ cups each

1 tablespoon reduced-calorie margarine

1 medium onion, thinly sliced

3 cups cut-up fully cooked smoked ham (about 1 pound)

4 small zucchini (about 1 pound), cut into julienne strips

1 green bell pepper, cut into ¼-inch strips

⅛ teaspoon pepper

¼ cup low-fat sour cream

¼ cup plain nonfat yogurt

1 teaspoon poppy seed

3 cups hot cooked noodles or rice

Heat margarine in 10-inch nonstick skillet. Cook onion, stirring occasionally, until softened. Stir in ham, zucchini, bell pepper and pepper. Cover and cook over medium heat about 8 minutes, stirring occasionally, until vegetables are crisp-tender.

Stir in sour cream, yogurt and poppy seed. Heat just until hot. Serve with noodles.

VEAL WITH SPINACH AND FETTUCCINE

———————	Per Serving	———————	
Calories	280	Fat	8 g (72 calories)
Protein	21 g	Cholesterol	85 mg
Carbohydrate	26 g	Sodium	360 mg

4 Servings, about ¾ cup veal mixture and ½ cup fettuccine each

¾ pound thin slices lean veal round steak or veal for scallopini

1 cup sliced mushrooms (about 3 ounces)

¼ cup chopped shallots or green onions with tops (about 3 medium)

½ cup Madeira wine or beef broth

½ cup beef broth

2 teaspoons cornstarch

⅛ teaspoon pepper

1 package (10 ounces) frozen chopped spinach, thawed and well drained

2 cups hot cooked fettuccine

Cut veal crosswise into ¼-inch strips. Spray 10-inch nonstick skillet with nonstick cooking spray. Sauté veal, mushrooms and shallots over medium-high heat 3 to 5 minutes or until veal is done.

Mix wine, broth, cornstarch and pepper. Stir wine mixture and spinach into skillet. Heat to boiling, stirring constantly. Boil and stir 1 minute. Serve over fettuccine.

CHAPTER 3
LIGHT OVEN MEALS

Mandarin-Almond Shrimp (page 36)

MANDARIN-ALMOND SHRIMP

Per Serving			
Calories	335	Fat 11 g (99 calories)	
Protein	19 g	Cholesterol	190 mg
Carbohydrate	41 g	Sodium	460 mg

6 Servings, about 1½ cups each

1 pound fresh or frozen raw medium shrimp (in shells)

2 cups boiling water

2 cups sliced mushrooms (about 5 ounces)

1 cup uncooked regular long grain rice

1 small onion, thinly sliced

1 teaspoon salt

¾ teaspoon ground ginger

1 cup whole almonds, toasted

1 can (15 ounces) mandarin orange segments, drained

1 package (6 ounces) frozen pea pods, thawed and drained

Peel shrimp. (If shrimp are frozen, do not thaw; peel in cold water.) Make a shallow cut lengthwise down back of each shrimp; wash out vein. Heat oven to 350°. Mix water, mushrooms, rice, onion, shrimp, salt and ginger in ungreased rectangular baking dish, 13×9×2 inches. Cover tightly with aluminum foil. Bake about 40 minutes or until liquid is absorbed and shrimp are pink.

Stir in remaining ingredients. Cover and let stand until pea pods are hot.

EASY FISH AND VEGETABLE PACKETS

Per Serving			
Calories	160	Fat 2 g (18 calories)	
Protein	25 g	Cholesterol	40 mg
Carbohydrate	7 g	Sodium	380 mg

4 Servings

4 frozen lean fish fillets (about 1 pound)

1 package (16 ounces) frozen broccoli, cauliflower and carrots

1 tablespoon chopped fresh or 1 teaspoon dried dill weed

½ teaspoon salt

¼ teaspoon pepper

4 tablespoons dry white wine

Heat oven to 450°. Place each frozen fish fillet on 12-inch square of aluminum foil. Top each fish fillet with one-fourth of the vegetables; sprinkle with dill weed, salt and pepper. Pour 1 tablespoon wine over each. Fold up sides of foil to make tent; fold top edges over to seal. Fold in sides, making a packet; fold to seal. Place packets on cookie sheet. Bake about 40 minutes or until vegetables are crisp-tender and fish flakes easily with fork.

BROILED CARIBBEAN SWORDFISH

If you can't find papayas, fresh or frozen (thawed) peaches make a delectable substitute.

———————	Per Serving	———————
Calories	310	Fat 9 g (81 calories)
Protein	44 g	Cholesterol 85 mg
Carbohydrate	11 g	Sodium 540 mg

4 Servings, with about ½ cup salsa each

Papaya Salsa (right)

4 swordfish, shark or other medium-fat fish steaks, 1 inch thick (about 1½ pounds)

1 tablespoon grated lime peel

¼ cup lime juice

¼ cup grapefruit juice

½ teaspoon salt

1 clove garlic, crushed

Prepare Papaya Salsa; cover and refrigerate. Place fish steaks in ungreased square baking dish, 8×8×2 inches. Mix remaining ingredients; pour over fish. Cover and refrigerate 2 hours.

Set oven control to broil. Spray broiler pan rack with nonstick cooking spray. Remove fish from marinade; reserve marinade. Place fish on rack in broiler pan. Broil with tops about 4 inches from heat about 16 minutes, turning and brushing with marinade after 8 minutes, until fish flakes easily with fork. Serve with salsa.

PAPAYA SALSA

1 large papaya, peeled, seeded and chopped (about 2 cups)

¼ cup finely chopped red bell pepper (about ½ small)

1 tablespoon finely chopped green onion with top (about ½ medium)

1 tablespoon chopped fresh cilantro

2 to 3 tablespoons grapefruit juice

⅛ teaspoon salt

Mix all ingredients.

If YOU LIKE CHICKEN but are trying to cut calories, there's a good chance you've passed up preparing or eating greasy fried chicken. However, you can indulge in fried chicken occasionally if you remove the skin before eating.

Making the switch from a fried chicken breast to a skinless broiled chicken breast saves about 80 calories for a 3-ounce portion. You save about 40 calories by broiling instead of frying and another 40 calories by removing the skin! You'll also find that the same size serving of light chicken meat has less fat than dark chicken meat.

Chicken can be purchased in a variety of ways: whole or cut-up whole, specific parts, skinned and boned, canned and cooked from the deli. It's versatile enough to be used at any meal, healthful and low in calories, and you'll find plenty of tempting flavorful recipes for this favorite right here.

CHICKEN WITH BLACK BEANS

Per Serving			
Calories	310	Fat 12 g (108 calories)	
Protein	28 g	Cholesterol	80 mg
Carbohydrate	22 g	Sodium	210 mg

4 Servings

4 chicken drumsticks (about 1 pound)

4 chicken thighs (about 1 pound)

2 cans (15 ounces each) black beans, undrained

1 tablespoon grated gingerroot or 1 teaspoon ground ginger

1 teaspoon finely shredded lime peel

2 tablespoons lime juice

½ teaspoon salt

1 clove garlic, finely chopped

1 cup cubed mango (about 1 medium) or 1 can (8 ounces) peach slices, drained and cut up

¼ cup thinly sliced green onions with tops (about 2 medium)

Heat oven to 375°. Place chicken pieces, skin sides up, in ungreased rectangular baking dish, 13 × 9 × 2 inches. Bake uncovered 40 minutes. Remove excess fat. Mix remaining ingredients. Spoon around chicken pieces. Cover and bake 30 minutes longer or until juices of chicken run clear.

GINGERED CHICKEN WITH PEA PODS

A whole chicken roasts best with the skin on, and you can easily remove the skin before serving; that's the way we recommend eating it. Therefore the calories were calculated for this dish without the skin, saving 200 calories a serving!

Per Serving			
Calories	300	Fat 11 g (99 calories)	
Protein	31 g	Cholesterol	90 mg
Carbohydrate	18 g	Sodium	540 mg

6 Servings

3- to 3½-pound whole broiler-fryer chicken

¼ teaspoon paprika

¼ teaspoon ground ginger

1 package (6 ounces) frozen Chinese pea pods

½ cup chopped onion (about 1 medium)

½ teaspoon ground turmeric

¼ teaspoon ground ginger

2 tablespoons reduced-calorie margarine

8 ounces medium whole mushrooms

1 teaspoon salt

2 teaspoons lemon juice

9 cherry tomatoes, cut into halves

Heat oven to 375°. Fold wings of chicken across back with tips touching. Tie drumsticks to tail. Place chicken, breast side up, on rack in shallow roasting pan. Sprinkle with paprika and ¼ teaspoon ginger. Roast uncovered about 1 hour 15 minutes, until juices of thickest parts run clear and drumstick meat feels very soft.

About 15 minutes before chicken is done, rinse pea pods with cold water to separate; drain. Cook onion, turmeric and ¼ teaspoon ginger in margarine in 10-inch skillet over medium heat about 3 minutes, stirring occasionally, until onion is softened. Stir in pea pods, mushrooms, salt and lemon juice. Cook uncovered about 5 minutes, stirring occasionally, until pea pods are hot. Stir in tomatoes; heat just until hot. Serve vegetables with chicken.

CHICKEN WITH PEPPERS AND ONIONS

Per Serving			
Calories	300	Fat 11 g (99 calories)	
Protein	31 g	Cholesterol	90 mg
Carbohydrate	18 g	Sodium	540 mg

6 Servings

3 pounds broiler-fryer chicken pieces, skinned

1 teaspoon Italian seasoning

¼ teaspoon salt

¼ teaspoon pepper

2 medium green bell peppers, cut into ¼-inch strips

2 medium onions, thinly sliced

1 cup sliced mushrooms (about 3 ounces) or 1 can (4 ounces) mushroom stems and pieces, drained

1 jar (15.5 ounces) spaghetti sauce

Heat oven to 375°. Remove excess fat from chicken; place chicken, meaty sides up, in rectangular pan, 13 × 9 × 2 inches. Sprinkle with Italian seasoning, salt and pepper. Mix remaining ingredients; spread over chicken. Cover and bake 30 minutes. Spoon sauce over chicken. Bake uncovered about 45 minutes, spooning sauce over chicken occasionally, until juices of thickest pieces of chicken run clear.

CHICKEN-RICE CASSEROLE

Per Serving			
Calories	290	Fat 12 g (108 calories)	
Protein	19 g	Cholesterol	40 mg
Carbohydrate	25 g	Sodium	520 mg

6 Servings, about 1 cup each

¼ cup reduced-calorie margarine

⅓ cup all-purpose flour

¾ teaspoon salt

⅛ teaspoon pepper

1½ cups skim milk

1 cup chicken broth

2 cups cut-up cooked chicken or turkey (about 10 ounces)

1½ cups cooked white rice or wild rice

⅓ cup chopped green bell pepper

¼ cup slivered almonds

2 tablespoons chopped pimiento

1 can (4 ounces) mushroom stems and pieces, drained

Heat oven to 350°. Heat margarine in 2-quart saucepan over medium heat. Stir in flour, salt and pepper. Cook, stirring constantly, until bubbly; remove from heat. Stir in milk and broth. Heat to boiling, stirring constantly. Boil and stir 1 minute. Stir in remaining ingredients.

Pour into ungreased 2-quart casserole or square baking dish, 8 × 8 × 2 inches. Bake uncovered 40 to 45 minutes or until bubbly. Garnish with parsley if desired.

If **YOU LIKE CASSEROLES,** try eliminating hidden calories by making the following substitutions:

For:	Substitute:	For:	Substitute:
Margarine or butter (1 tablespoon = 100 calories)	Reduced-calorie margarine (1 tablespoon = 50 calories)	Cheddar cheese (1 cup shredded [4 ounces] = 460 calories)	Low-fat Cheddar cheese (1 cup shredded [4 ounces] = 200 calories)
Tuna canned in oil (6 ounces = 340 calories)	Tuna canned in water (6 ounces = 220 calories)	Whole milk (1 cup = 160 calories)	Skim milk (1 cup = 90 calories)
Almonds or peanuts (½ cup = 430 calories)	Water chestnuts (½ cup sliced = 70 calories)		

SCALLOPED POTATOES AND HAM

Per Serving			
Calories	180	Fat	6 g (54 calories)
Protein	14 g	Cholesterol	15 mg
Carbohydrate	15 g	Sodium	720 mg

4 Servings, about 1 cup each

2 tablespoons reduced-calorie margarine

3 tablespoons all-purpose flour

½ teaspoon dry mustard

¼ teaspoon salt

⅛ teaspoon pepper

2 cups skim milk

3 cups thinly sliced pared potatoes (about 3 medium)

1 cup diced fully cooked smoked extra-lean ham (about 6 ounces)

¼ cup finely chopped onion (about 1 small)

Heat oven to 350°. Spray 1½-quart casserole with nonstick cooking spray. Heat margarine in 1½-quart saucepan over medium heat. Stir in flour, mustard, salt and pepper. Cook, stirring constantly, until margarine is absorbed. Gradually stir in milk. Heat to boiling, stirring constantly. Boil and stir 1 minute.

Layer one-third of the potatoes, half of the ham, half of the onion and one-third of the sauce in casserole; repeat. Top with remaining potatoes and sauce. Cover and bake 30 minutes. Uncover and bake about 40 minutes or until potatoes are tender. Let stand 5 to 10 minutes before serving.

BROILED VEAL AND ONIONS

If onions won't stand upright, cut a thin slice off the small end of each onion.

	Per Serving		
Calories	350	Fat 12 g (108 calories)	
Protein	45 g	Cholesterol	130 mg
Carbohydrate	13 g	Sodium	300 mg

4 Servings

4 veal rib or loin chops, about ¾ inch thick

1 tablespoon Dijon mustard

1 teaspoon mustard seed

¼ teaspoon salt

¼ teaspoon pepper

2 large yellow onions (about 3 inches in diameter), cut into halves

4 teaspoons reduced-calorie margarine, softened

2 tablespoons packed brown sugar

¼ teaspoon pepper

Set oven control to broil. Brush both sides of veal chops lightly with mustard; sprinkle with mustard seed, salt and ¼ teaspoon pepper.

Place veal and onions, cut sides down, on rack in broiler pan. Broil with tops of veal about 3 inches from heat about 6 minutes or until veal is brown; turn veal and onions. Spread 1 teaspoon margarine over each onion half; sprinkle with brown sugar and ¼ teaspoon pepper. Broil about 6 minutes longer or until veal is brown and onions are tender.

Sweet-and-Sour Turkey Patties

For extra crunch, serve patties on crisp rice cakes.

		Per Serving		
Calories	315	Fat	9 g (81 calories)	
Protein	27 g	Cholesterol	75 mg	
Carbohydrate	30 g	Sodium	290 mg	

6 Servings, with about ⅓ cup sauce each

1½ pounds ground turkey

1 cup soft bread crumbs (about 1½ slices bread)

⅓ cup chicken broth

1 can (8 ounces) crushed pineapple in juice, drained and juice reserved

3 tablespoons sugar

¼ cup vinegar

1 teaspoon soy sauce

1 small clove garlic, finely chopped

2 tablespoons cornstarch

2 tablespoons cold water

½ cup chopped bell pepper (about 1 small)

Set oven control to broil. Mix ground turkey, bread crumbs and broth. Shape mixture into 6 patties, each about ½ inch thick. Place on rack in broiler pan. Broil with tops about 3 inches from heat about 6 minutes on each side or until no longer pink.

Add enough water to reserved pineapple juice to measure 1 cup. Heat pineapple juice mixture, sugar, vinegar, soy sauce and garlic to boiling in 2-quart saucepan. Mix cornstarch and water; stir into juice mixture. Boil and stir 1 minute. Stir in pineapple and bell pepper. Serve sauce over patties.

TURKEY PIZZA

Per Serving			
Calories	295	Fat 12 g (108 calories)	
Protein	29 g	Cholesterol	70 mg
Carbohydrate	17 g	Sodium	510 mg

6 Servings

5 slices whole wheat bread, torn into small pieces

1 egg white, beaten

1 can (8 ounces) pizza sauce

1 pound ground turkey

½ cup chopped onion (about 1 medium)

1 teaspoon Italian seasoning

2 cloves garlic, crushed

1 cup sliced mushrooms (about 3 ounces) or 1 can (4 ounces) mushroom stems and pieces, drained

½ cup chopped green bell pepper (about 1 small)

2 cups shredded low-fat mozzarella cheese (8 ounces)

Heat oven to 375°. Spray rectangular pan, 13 × 9 × 2 inches, or 12-inch pizza pan with nonstick cooking spray. Mix bread and egg white. Pat firmly in pan, dipping fingers in water, if necessary, to prevent sticking. Bake 10 minutes or until crust feels firm. Spread pizza sauce evenly over crust.

Cook ground turkey, onion, Italian seasoning and garlic in 10-inch skillet over medium-high heat until turkey is no longer pink; drain. Sprinkle turkey mixture over pizza sauce. Top with mushrooms, bell pepper and cheese. Bake 15 to 20 minutes or until cheese is melted.

ZUCCHINI LASAGNE

Per Serving			
Calories	230	Fat 12 g (108 calories)	
Protein	15 g	Cholesterol	35 mg
Carbohydrate	16 g	Sodium	240 mg

8 Servings

3 cups chunky-style spaghetti sauce

1 cup shredded zucchini (about 1 medium)

6 uncooked lasagne noodles

1 cup ricotta or small curd creamed cottage cheese

¼ cup grated Parmesan cheese

1 tablespoon chopped fresh or 1 teaspoon dried oregano leaves

2 cups shredded mozzarella cheese (8 ounces)

Heat oven to 350°. Mix spaghetti sauce and zucchini. Spread 1 cup mixture in ungreased rectangular baking dish, 11 × 7 × 1½ inches. Top with 3 noodles. Mix ricotta cheese, Parmesan cheese and oregano; spread over noodles in dish. Spread with 1 cup of the sauce mixture.

Top with remaining noodles, sauce mixture and mozzarella cheese. Bake uncovered about 45 minutes or until hot and bubbly. Let stand 15 minutes before cutting.

Cheddar Strata with Grilled Onions

Per Serving			
Calories	235	Fat 7 g (63 calories)	
Protein	17 g	Cholesterol	155 mg
Carbohydrate	26 g	Sodium	760 mg

6 Servings

1 teaspoon vegetable oil

2 medium onions, sliced

8 slices rye bread

2 tablespoons Dijon mustard

1½ cups shredded low-fat Cheddar cheese (6 ounces)

1 cup coarsley chopped seeded tomato (about 1 medium)

1½ cups skim milk

4 eggs

Heat oven to 300°. Heat oil in 10-inch nonstick skillet over medium-high heat. Sauté onions 6 to 8 minutes or until golden brown.

Spray square baking dish, 8×8×2 inches, with nonstick cooking spray. Trim crusts from bread. Spread mustard on one side of each slice bread. Arrange 4 slices bread, mustard side up, in dish. Layer 1 cup of the cheese, the tomato and onions on bread. Place remaining bread slices, mustard side down, on onions.

Beat milk and eggs until well blended. Pour evenly over bread. Bake immediately, or cover and refrigerate up to 24 hours.

Bake uncovered about 1 hour or until center is set and bread is golden brown. Sprinkle with remaining ½ cup cheese. Let stand 10 minutes before cutting.

Confetti Rice Casserole

Per Serving			
Calories	335	Fat 13 g (117 calories)	
Protein	15 g	Cholesterol	170 mg
Carbohydrate	39 g	Sodium	660 mg

6 Servings, about 1 cup each

6 ounces process sharp American or Swiss cheese or process cheese spread loaf, cut into ½-inch cubes

⅓ cup milk

4 hard-cooked eggs, sliced

3 cups cooked rice

1 package (10 ounces) frozen mixed vegetables, thawed

½ cup chopped onion (about 1 medium)

½ teaspoon salt

Heat oven to 350°. Heat cheese and milk in 3-quart saucepan over low heat about 5 minutes, stirring constantly, until cheese is melted. Reserve 3 to 5 egg slices. Stir remaining egg slices and remaining ingredients into cheese sauce. Pour into ungreased rectangular baking dish, 11×7×1½ inches, or 1½-quart casserole. Bake uncovered 25 to 30 minutes or until hot and bubbly. Garnish with reserved egg slices and, if desired, fresh parsley.

CHAPTER 4
GUILT-FREE PASTA

Triple-Cheese Ravioli (page 75)

If YOU LOVE PASTA and want to keep your calorie count low, try the following suggestions:

▲ Mix cooked vegetables with pasta for a hot main dish and raw for a cold salad.

▲ A 1-cup serving of pasta contains about 200 calories. Substitute ½ cup of cut-up, low-calorie vegetables for ½ cup of the pasta, and you'll cut your calorie count to 120. See Vegetables under "Counting Calories" (page 148) for vegetable suggestions.

▲ Toss equal parts of cooked spaghetti with cooked spaghetti squash for great flavor.

SALMON WITH CUCUMBER SAUCE

Per Serving			
Calories	225	Fat	4 g (36 calories)
Protein	17 g	Cholesterol	20 mg
Carbohydrate	29 g	Sodium	310 mg

4 Servings, about 1 cup each

½ pound salmon fillets or other fatty

1 cup plain nonfat yogurt

1 tablespoon all-purpose flour

1 tablespoon chopped fresh or 1 teaspoon dried dill weed

1 teaspoon prepared horseradish

1 cup chopped seeded unpared cucumber (about 1 medium)

1 cup uncooked medium shell (conchiglie) or seashell macaroni (about 4 ounces)

Place salmon fillets in 2-quart saucepan; add enough water to cover. Heat to boiling; reduce heat. Simmer uncovered 6 to 8 minutes or until fish flakes easily with fork. Remove fish with slotted spatula; drain. Remove any skin. Flake fish into bite-size pieces; keep warm.

Mix yogurt and flour in same 2-quart saucepan. Stir in dill weed and horseradish. Heat over low heat until hot (do not boil). Stir in cucumber and fish. Cook macaroni as directed on package; drain. Serve sauce over macaroni. Garnish with thinly sliced cucumber if desired.

1 can (6¾ ounces) skinless boneless pink salmon, drained and flaked, can be substituted for the salmon fillets. Do not cook.

SCAMPI WITH FETTUCCINE

————	Per Serving	————
Calories	335	Fat 12 g (108 calories)
Protein	24 g	Cholesterol 335 mg
Carbohydrate	32 g	Sodium 290 mg

4 Servings, about 1 cup each

1½ pounds fresh or frozen raw medium shrimp (in shells)

6 ounces uncooked spinach fettuccine

2 tablespoons olive or vegetable oil

2 tablespoons thinly sliced green onions with tops

1 tablespoon chopped fresh or 1½ teaspoons dried basil leaves

1 tablespoon chopped fresh parsley

2 tablespoons lemon juice

2 cloves garlic, finely chopped

¼ teaspoon salt

Peel shrimp. (If shrimp are frozen, do not thaw; peel in cold water.) Make a shallow cut lengthwise down back of each shrimp; wash out vein. Cook fettuccine as directed on package; drain.

Heat oil in 10-inch skillet over medium heat. Stir in shrimp and remaining ingredients. Cook, stirring frequently, 2 to 3 minutes or until shrimp are pink; remove from heat. Toss fettuccine with shrimp mixture in skillet.

SOUTHWEST SCALLOPS

Can't find Anaheim chilies? Use a small red bell pepper. It will also give the sauce a milder and sweeter flavor.

————	Per Serving	————
Calories	335	Fat 6 g (54 calories)
Protein	39 g	Cholesterol 80 mg
Carbohydrate	34 g	Sodium 430 mg

6 Servings, about 1¼ cups each

1 red Anaheim chili, chopped

¼ cup sliced green onions with tops (about 3 medium)

2 tablespoons reduced-calorie margarine

2 tablespoons lime juice

2 pounds sea scallops

2 cups cubed fresh pineapple

1 cup Chinese pea pod halves (about 3 ounces)

3 cups hot cooked fettuccine

Cook chili, onions, margarine and lime juice in 10-inch skillet, stirring occasionally, until margarine is melted. Carefully stir in scallops. Cook over medium heat about 12 minutes, stirring frequently, until scallops are white. Stir in pineapple and pea pods. Heat until hot. Remove scallop mixture with slotted spoon; keep warm.

Heat liquid in skillet to boiling. Boil until slightly thickened and reduced to about half. Spoon scallop mixture onto fettuccine; pour liquid over scallop mixture.

CAJUN SEAFOOD AND NOODLES

If frozen shrimp and crab are not readily available, canned shrimp and crab are just as delicious.

Per Serving			
Calories	225	Fat	5 g (45 calories)
Protein	15 g	Cholesterol	85 mg
Carbohydrate	31 g	Sodium	240 mg

6 Servings, about ⅔ cup fish mixture and ½ cup noodles each

6 ounces uncooked medium noodles (about 3 cups)

1 tablespoon vegetable oil

¾ cup chopped green bell pepper (about 1 medium)

½ cup chopped onion (about 1 medium)

2 tablespoons chopped fresh parsley

⅛ teaspoon ground red pepper (cayenne)

⅛ teaspoon pepper

2 cloves garlic, finely chopped

1 tablespoon all-purpose flour

1 can (16 ounces) whole tomatoes, undrained

1 package (10 ounces) frozen cut okra, thawed

1 package (6 ounces) frozen cooked small shrimp, thawed and drained

1 package (6 ounces) frozen crabmeat, thawed, drained and cartilage removed

Cook noodles as directed on package; drain. Heat oil in 10-inch nonstick skillet over medium heat. Cook bell pepper, onion, parsley, red pepper, pepper and garlic 3 minutes, stirring frequently. Stir in flour and tomatoes; break up tomatoes.

Cook uncovered, stirring frequently, until mixture thickens and boils. Stir in okra, shrimp and crabmeat. Cook uncovered 5 minutes, stirring occasionally. Serve over noodles.

CHICKEN-BASIL NOODLES

	Per Serving		
Calories	280	Fat	8 g (72 calories)
Protein	24 g	Cholesterol	60 mg
Carbohydrate	28 g	Sodium	330 mg

4 Servings, about ¾ cup chicken mixture
and ½ cup noodles each

2 teaspoons olive or vegetable oil

½ cup finely chopped onion (about 1 medium)

1 clove garlic, finely chopped

2½ cups chopped tomatoes (about 3 medium)

2 cups cubed cooked chicken or turkey

¼ cup chopped fresh or 1 tablespoon dried basil leaves

½ teaspoon salt

⅛ teaspoon red pepper sauce

4 ounces uncooked noodles (about 2 cups)

Heat oil in 10-inch nonstick skillet over medium-high heat. Cook onion and garlic in oil until softened. Stir in remaining ingredients except noodles; reduce heat to medium. Cover and cook about 5 minutes, stirring frequently, until mixture is hot and tomatoes are soft. Cook noodles as directed on package; drain. Serve chicken mixture over noodles.

PASTA SHELLS WITH CHICKEN AND BROCCOLI

For variety, try different shapes and flavors of pasta. Use similar size pastas, so cooking time is consistent.

	Per Serving		
Calories	325	Fat 12 g (108 calories)	
Protein	20 g	Cholesterol	40 mg
Carbohydrate	33 g	Sodium	490 mg

6 Servings, about 1½ cups each

6 ounces uncooked macaroni shells or wheels

1 cup chopped broccoli

⅓ cup chopped onion (about 1 medium)

2 cloves garlic, finely chopped

1 carrot, cut into very thin strips

2 tablespoons vegetable oil

2 cups cut-up cooked chicken or turkey

1 teaspoon salt

2 large tomatoes, chopped (about 2 cups)

⅓ cup grated Parmesan cheese

2 tablespoons chopped fresh parsley

Cook macaroni as directed on package; drain. Cook broccoli, onion, garlic and carrot in oil in 10-inch skillet over medium heat about 10 minutes, stirring occasionally, until broccoli is crisp-tender.

Stir in chicken, salt and tomatoes. Cook uncovered about 3 minutes or just until chicken is hot. Spoon over macaroni. Sprinkle with cheese and parsley.

Pasta Shells with Chicken and Broccoli

If YOU VARY PASTA SHAPES, be sure to substitute measure for measure, in similar sizes. For recipes that call for a specific amount of uncooked pasta, substitutions might be difficult because of variations in weight. Use the following pasta guide to figure out how much to prepare. Don't forget to factor in the low-calorie substitutions (page 52).

Type	Uncooked	Cooked
Macaroni	6 or 7 ounces (2 cups)	4 cups
Rotini	8 ounces	6 cups
Spaghetti	7 or 8 ounces	4 cups
Noodles	8 ounces	4 to 5 cups

FARFALLE WITH CILANTRO PESTO

Per Serving

Calories	270	Fat 11 g (99 calories)	
Protein	16 g	Cholesterol	30 mg
Carbohydrate	28 g	Sodium	100 mg

4 Servings, about 1¾ cups each

6 ounces uncooked farfalle (bow-tie pasta)

2 tablespoons olive oil

3 tablespoons nonfat plain yogurt

2 teaspoons lime juice

¼ cup grated Parmesan cheese

1 tablespoon slivered almonds, toasted

2 cloves garlic

⅛ teaspoon pepper

1 cup firmly packed fresh cilantro

2 teaspoons olive oil

1½ cups cut-up cooked chicken or turkey (about 8 ounces)

3 cups cubed yellow squash or zucchini (about 2 medium)

8 cherry tomatoes, each cut into fourths

Cook farfalle as directed on package; drain.

Place 2 tablespoons oil, the yogurt, lime juice, cheese, almonds, garlic, pepper and cilantro in blender in order listed. Cover and blend on medium speed about 2 minutes, stopping blender occasionally to scrape sides, until almost smooth.

Heat 2 teaspoons oil in 10-inch nonstick skillet over medium heat. Cook chicken and squash about 5 minutes, stirring frequently, until squash is tender. Stir in cilantro mixture, farfalle and tomatoes. Heat until hot.

LINGUINE WITH CHICKEN AND ARTICHOKE HEARTS

Per Serving			
Calories	350	Fat	9 g (81 calories)
Protein	28 g	Cholesterol	65 mg
Carbohydrate	42 g	Sodium	260 mg

4 Servings, about 1½ cups each

1 jar (6 ounces) marinated artichoke hearts

1 tablespoon olive or vegetable oil

½ cup coarsely chopped onion (about 1 medium)

2 cups cut-up cooked chicken or turkey (about 10 ounces)

1 cup frozen green peas

2 ounces sliced fully cooked extra-lean smoked ham, cut into ¼-inch strips (about ½ cup)*

1 tablespoon snipped fresh or 1 teaspoon dried oregano leaves

¼ teaspoon pepper

1 container (8 ounces) low-fat sour cream (1 cup)

6 ounces uncooked linguine or spaghetti

Drain liquid from artichoke hearts into 10-inch skillet. Cut artichoke hearts in half and reserve. Add oil to artichoke liquid. Cook onion in oil mixture, stirring occasionally, until softened.

Stir artichoke hearts, chicken, peas, ham, oregano and pepper into onion mixture. Cook, stirring occasionally, until hot; remove from heat. Stir in sour cream. Cover and keep warm. Cook linguine as directed on package; drain. Toss linguine with sauce.

*6 slices bacon, crisply cooked and crumbled, can be substituted for the ham.

TARRAGON AND CHICKEN PASTA

Tarragon with its distinctive, aniselike flavor is a marvelous seasoning for chicken, fish and vegetables.

——————— Per Serving ———————			
Calories	315	Fat	7 g (63 calories)
Protein	27 g	Cholesterol	55 mg
Carbohydrate	35 g	Sodium	280 mg

4 Servings, about 1¼ cups each

1 cup uncooked spiral macaroni (about 4 ounces)

2 cups sliced mushrooms (about 5 ounces)

1 cup broccoli flowerets

1 cup thinly sliced carrots (about 2 large)

1 cup skim milk

1 tablespoon cornstarch

2 teaspoons chopped fresh or ½ teaspoon dried tarragon leaves

¼ teaspoon salt

1 clove garlic, finely chopped

2 cups shredded spinach or romaine lettuce (about 3 ounces)

1½ cups cut-up cooked chicken or turkey (about 8 ounces)

½ cup shredded Swiss cheese (2 ounces)

Cook macaroni as directed on package—except add mushrooms, broccoli and carrots during last 4 minutes of cooking; drain.

Mix milk, cornstarch, tarragon, salt and garlic in 1½-quart saucepan. Cook over medium heat 4 minutes, stirring constantly, until mixture thickens and boils. Stir in remaining ingredients until cheese is melted and spinach is wilted. Toss with macaroni mixture.

Tarragon and Chicken Pasta

MEXICAN CHICKEN MANICOTTI

Per Serving			
Calories	350	Fat 12 g (108 calories)	
Protein	29 g	Cholesterol	75 mg
Carbohydrate	32 g	Sodium	180 mg

4 Servings, 2 manicotti each

8 uncooked manicotti shells

1½ cups cut-up cooked chicken or turkey (about 8 ounces)

1 cup shredded carrot (about 2 medium)

1 cup low-fat ricotta cheese

2 tablespoons sliced green onions with tops

2 tablespoons chopped fresh or 2 teaspoons dried cilantro

1 clove garlic, finely chopped

1 cup salsa

¼ cup shredded Monterey Jack cheese with jalapeño peppers (1 ounce)

Heat oven to 325°. Cook manicotti shells as directed on package; drain. Mix chicken, carrot, ricotta cheese, onions, cilantro and garlic. Fill manicotti shells with chicken mixture.

Arrange in ungreased rectangular pan, 13×9×2 inches. Pour salsa over manicotti; sprinkle with Monterey Jack cheese. Cover and bake about 35 minutes or until hot in center.

TURKEY-PASTA PRIMAVERA

Per Serving			
Calories	300	Fat 9 g (81 calories)	
Protein	21 g	Cholesterol	75 mg
Carbohydrate	34 g	Sodium	670 mg

6 Servings, about ⅔ cup turkey mixture and ⅔ cup spaghetti each

6 ounces uncooked spaghetti or fettuccine

1 cup chopped broccoli

⅓ cup chopped onion

2 cloves garlic, finely chopped

½ cup julienne strips carrot (about 1 medium)

1 tablespoon vegetable oil

2 cups cut-up cooked turkey or chicken

1 teaspoon salt

2 cups chopped tomatoes (about 2 large)

⅓ cup freshly grated Parmesan cheese

2 tablespoons chopped fresh parsley

Cook spaghetti as directed on package; drain.

Cook broccoli, onion, garlic and carrot in oil in 10-inch nonstick skillet over medium heat about 10 minutes, stirring occasionally, until broccoli is crisp-tender.

Stir in turkey, salt and tomatoes. Heat about 3 minutes or just until turkey is hot. Spoon over spaghetti. Sprinkle with cheese and parsley.

CURRIED TURKEY SPAGHETTI

Curry is a catchall term used to refer to many types of spicy sauces, all of which have curry powder as a dominant ingredient. To vary this curry, try spinach or whole wheat pasta.

———————	Per Serving	———————
Calories	350	Fat 8 g (72 calories)
Protein	21 g	Cholesterol 35 mg
Carbohydrate	50 g	Sodium 260 mg

4 Servings, about 1¼ cups each

- **½ pound ground turkey or lean ground beef**
- **½ cup chopped onion (about 1 medium)**
- **1 clove garlic, finely chopped**
- **¾ cup chopped unpared tart eating apple (about 1 medium)**
- **¼ cup chopped fresh parsley**
- **1½ teaspoons curry powder**
- **½ teaspoon ground cumin**
- **⅛ teaspoon ground red pepper (cayenne)**
- **¼ cup unsweetened apple juice**
- **1 can (16 ounces) whole tomatoes, undrained**
- **6 ounces uncooked spaghetti**
- **2 tablespoons chopped dry roasted peanuts**

Cook ground turkey, onion and garlic in 10-inch skillet over medium heat, stirring frequently, until turkey is no longer pink; drain. Stir in remaining ingredients except spaghetti and peanuts; break up tomatoes. Heat to boiling; reduce heat. Simmer uncovered about 5 minutes or until apple is tender, stirring occasionally.

Cook spaghetti as directed on package; drain. Serve sauce over spaghetti. Sprinkle with peanuts.

SPICY BEEF WITH CELLOPHANE NOODLES

Cellophane noodles aren't traditional pasta, but translucent threads made from the starch of green mung beans.

	Per Serving			
Calories	320	Fat	8 g (72 calories)	
Protein	34 g	Cholesterol	85 mg	
Carbohydrate	25 g	Sodium	740 mg	

4 Servings, about 1½ cups each

1 package (3¾ ounces) cellophane noodles

6 ounces fresh Chinese pea pods*

2 tablespoons soy sauce

2 tablespoons rice wine vinegar

2 teaspoons grated gingerroot or ½ teaspoon ground ginger

1 teaspoon cornstarch

2 teaspoons honey

½ teaspoon crushed red pepper

¼ teaspoon salt

1-pound lean beef boneless round steak

1 teaspoon sesame oil

2 cloves garlic, finely chopped

1 teaspoon sesame oil

1 cup thinly sliced carrots (about 2 large)

1 can (8 ounces) sliced water chestnuts, drained

Cover noodles with hot water. Let stand 10 minutes; drain. Remove strings from pea pods. Place pea pods in boiling water in 2-quart saucepan. Cover and cook 1 minute; drain. Immediately rinse with cold water; drain. Mix soy sauce, vinegar, gingerroot, cornstarch, honey, red pepper and salt; reserve.

Trim fat from beef steak. Cut beef with grain into 2-inch strips. Cut strips across grain into ⅛-inch slices. (For ease in cutting, partially freeze beef, about 1 hour.) Heat 1 teaspoon sesame oil in 10-inch nonstick skillet over medium-high heat. Add beef and garlic; stir-fry about 3 minutes or until beef is no longer pink. Remove beef from skillet. Add 1 teaspoon sesame oil to skillet. Add carrots and water chestnuts; stir-fry about 1 minute or until carrots are crisp-tender. Stir in beef mixture and cornstarch mixture; cook and stir about 30 seconds or until thickened. Stir in pea pods; cook and stir 30 seconds. Serve over noodles.

*1 package (6 ounces) frozen Chinese pea pods, thawed and drained, can be substituted for the fresh pea pods. Do not remove strings or cook.

Spicy Beef with Cellophane Noodles (page 65)
Sauerbraten Meatballs and Noodles (page 68)

Sauerbraten Meatballs and Noodles

Per Serving			
Calories	300	Fat	7 g (63 calories)
Protein	24 g	Cholesterol	85 mg
Carbohydrate	34 g	Sodium	480 mg

6 Servings, 4 meatballs and about
¾ cup noodles each

1 pound lean ground beef or pork

⅓ cup crushed gingersnaps (about 6 gingersnaps)

½ cup finely chopped onion (about 1 medium)

¼ cup water

½ teaspoon salt

¼ teaspoon pepper

6 ounces uncooked egg noodles or spaetzle (about 3 cups)

1 cup beef broth

¼ cup apple cider vinegar

1 tablespoon sugar

¼ cup crushed gingersnaps (about 4 gingersnaps)

2 tablespoons raisins

Heat oven to 400°. Mix ground beef, ⅓ cup gingersnaps, the onion, water, salt and pepper. Shape mixture into 24 meatballs. Spray rack in broiler pan with nonstick cooking spray. Place meatballs on rack. Bake uncovered 20 to 25 minutes or until done and light brown.

Cook noodles as directed on package; drain. Mix remaining ingredients except raisins in 1½-quart saucepan. Cook over medium heat, stirring constantly, until mixture thickens and boils. Stir in raisins and meatballs. Heat until hot. Serve over noodles.

PORK AND PASTA STIR-FRY

Great for leftover pasta! If you use cold pasta, it will take a bit longer to heat when added to the stir-fry.

--------- Per Serving ---------

Calories	315	Fat 18 g (162 calories)	
Protein	20 g	Cholesterol	75 mg
Carbohydrate	18 g	Sodium	460 mg

6 Servings, about 1 cup each

- **1¼ pounds lean pork boneless loin or leg**
- **1 teaspoon cornstarch**
- **1 teaspoon soy sauce**
- **¼ teaspoon salt**
- **⅛ teaspoon pepper**
- **2 tablespoons vegetable oil**
- **2 large cloves garlic, finely chopped**
- **¼ to ½ teaspoon crushed red pepper**
- **1 cup ¼-inch diagonal slices celery (about 2 medium stalks)**
- **1 small green or red bell pepper, cut into 1-inch pieces**
- **2 cups bean sprouts (about 4 ounces)**
- **1½ cups sliced mushrooms (about 4 ounces)**
- **2 cups cooked vermicelli**
- **¼ cup sliced green onions with tops (about 3 medium)**
- **1 tablespoon soy sauce**

Trim fat from pork loin; cut pork with grain into 2-inch strips. Cut strips across grain into ⅛-inch slices. (For ease in cutting, partially freeze pork, about 1½ hours.) Toss pork, cornstarch, 1 teaspoon soy sauce, the salt and pepper. Cover and refrigerate 20 minutes.

Heat oil in 12-inch nonstick skillet or wok over high heat. Add pork, garlic and red pepper; stir-fry about 5 minutes or until pork is no longer pink. Add celery and bell pepper; stir-fry 2 minutes. Add bean sprouts and mushrooms; stir-fry 2 minutes. Add remaining ingredients; toss about 2 minutes or until thoroughly mixed and hot.

Pastitsio

Our recipe was inspired by the classic Greek pastitsio, layered with pasta, spiced meat and custard.

Per Serving			
Calories	240	Fat 6 g (54 calories)	
Protein	23 g	Cholesterol	80 mg
Carbohydrate	24 g	Sodium	440 mg

6 Servings, about 1 cup each

1 cup uncooked elbow macaroni (about 4 ounces)

1 egg white

¼ cup grated Parmesan cheese

2 tablespoons skim milk

¾ pound lean ground lamb or beef

1½ cups cubed pared eggplant (1 small)

1 can (14½ ounces) whole tomatoes, drained

½ cup chopped onion (about 1 medium)

½ teaspoon salt

¼ teaspoon ground cinnamon

¼ teaspoon ground nutmeg

1 clove garlic, finely chopped

1 cup skim milk

1 tablespoon cornstarch

2 tablespoons grated Parmesan cheese

1 egg, beaten

Cook macaroni as directed on package; drain. Stir in egg white, ¼ cup cheese and 2 tablespoons milk

Cook ground lamb in 10-inch skillet over medium heat about 10 minutes or until no longer pink; drain. Stir in eggplant, tomatoes, onion, salt, cinnamon, nutmeg and garlic; break up tomatoes.

Heat oven to 350°. Cook 1 cup milk and the cornstarch in 1-quart saucepan over medium heat, stirring constantly, until mixture thickens and boils. Stir in remaining ingredients. Place half of the macaroni mixture in ungreased 1½-quart casserole. Top with lamb mixture, remaining macaroni mixture and the sauce. Bake uncovered about 40 minutes or until set in center.

MINTY LAMB STIR-FRY

Per Serving			
Calories	320	Fat	8 g (72 calories)
Protein	27 g	Cholesterol	105 mg
Carbohydrate	36 g	Sodium	210 mg

4 Servings, about ⅔ cup lamb mixture
and ½ cup pasta each

6 ounces uncooked angel hair pasta

½ cup mashed pared kiwifruit (about 2 medium)

1 tablespoon chopped fresh or 1 teaspoon dried mint leaves, crushed

1 teaspoon cornstarch

¼ teaspoon salt

1 tablespoon vegetable oil

¾ pound lean lamb boneless shoulder or leg, cut into 2 × ¼-inch strips

1 clove garlic, finely chopped

1 cup julienne strips carrots (about 2 medium)

1 cup julienne strips zucchini (about 5 ounces)

Cook pasta as directed on package; drain. Mix kiwifruit, mint, cornstarch and salt.

Heat oil in 10-inch nonstick skillet over medium-high heat. Stir-fry lamb and garlic about 3 minutes or until lamb is no longer pink. Add carrots and zucchini; stir-fry 2 minutes. Add kiwifruit mixture; stir-fry 1 minute. Serve over pasta.

THREE-CHEESE NOODLE BAKE

If you prefer to use regular rather than low-fat Cheddar cheese, add 50 calories per serving.

Per Serving			
Calories	275	Fat	9 g (81 calories)
Protein	22 g	Cholesterol	80 mg
Carbohydrate	25 g	Sodium	690 mg

4 Servings, about 1 cup each

4 ounces uncooked noodles (about 2 cups)

1 cup low-fat cottage cheese

¾ cup shredded low-fat Cheddar cheese (3 ounces)

½ cup low-fat sour cream

⅓ cup chopped green onions with tops

3 tablespoons grated Parmesan cheese

½ teaspoon Worcestershire sauce

⅛ teaspoon pepper

2 egg whites

1 egg

Heat oven to 350°. Spray square baking dish, 8 × 8 × 2 inches, with nonstick cooking spray. Cook noodles as directed on package; drain. Mix noodles and remaining ingredients. Spread in dish. Bake uncovered 30 to 35 minutes or until center is set and edges are golden brown. Let stand 5 minutes.

CREAMY MACARONI AND CHEESE

———— Per Serving ————			
Calories	210	Fat	4 g (36 calories)
Protein	17 g	Cholesterol	15 mg
Carbohydrate	26 g	Sodium	710 mg

6 Servings, about 1 cup each

1½ cups uncooked elbow or spiral macaroni (about 5 ounces)

¼ cup chopped onion (about 1 small)

1 clove garlic, finely chopped

1½ cups skim milk

1 tablespoon cornstarch

¼ teaspoon ground red pepper (cayenne)

¼ teaspoon salt

¼ teaspoon dry mustard

1½ cups shredded low-fat Cheddar cheese (6 ounces)

1 cup low-fat cottage cheese

1 cup chopped tomato (about 1 large), if desired

Cook macaroni as directed on package—except add onion and garlic to water and decrease cooking time to 4 minutes; drain.

Heat oven to 375°. Mix milk, cornstarch, red pepper, salt and mustard in 2-quart saucepan. Cook over medium heat, stirring constantly, until mixture thickens and boils. Boil and stir 1 minute; remove from heat. Stir in Cheddar cheese and cottage cheese. Stir in macaroni and tomato. Turn into ungreased 1½-quart casserole. Bake uncovered about 30 minutes or until light brown on top and bubbly around edges.

VERMICELLI WITH LEMONY GREEN VEGETABLES

————————— Per Serving —————————

Calories	350	Fat 11 g (99 calories)	
Protein	14 g	Cholesterol	20 mg
Carbohydrate	48 g	Sodium	470 mg

4 Servings, about 1½ cups each

1 package (7 ounces) uncooked vermicelli

4 cups mixed bite-size pieces green vegetables (asparagus, broccoli, Chinese pea pods, green beans, zucchini)

2 tablespoons reduced-calorie margarine

1 tablespoon grated lemon peel

½ cup skim milk

1 package (3 ounces) Neufchâtel cheese, cut into cubes and softened

⅓ cup grated Parmesan cheese

Salt and pepper to taste

Cook vermicelli as directed on package; drain. While vermicelli is cooking, cook vegetables in margarine in 10-inch skillet over medium heat about 7 minutes, stirring frequently, until crisp-tender. Toss with lemon peel. Remove vegetables; keep warm.

Heat milk and Neufchâtel cheese in skillet until smooth and creamy. Stir in Parmesan cheese, salt and pepper. Toss with vermicelli. Serve vegetables over vermicelli and, if desired, with lemon wedges and coarsely ground pepper.

VEGETABLE LASAGNE

This tasty lasagne is long on vegetables and short on noodles. For a quicker and equally delicious dish, try Zucchini Lasagne (page 47).

—————— Per Serving ——————			
Calories	200	Fat	9 g (81 calories)
Protein	14 g	Cholesterol	70 mg
Carbohydrate	16 g	Sodium	740 mg

6 Servings

Vegetable Sauce (right)

1 container (15 ounces) part-skim ricotta cheese

¼ cup grated Romano cheese

2 tablespoons chopped fresh parsley

1 egg

3 uncooked lasagne noodles

½ cup shredded mozzarella cheese (2 ounces)

2 tablespoons grated Romano cheese

Heat oven to 350°. Spray rectangular baking dish, 10 × 6 × 1½ inches, with nonstick cooking spray. Prepare Vegetable Sauce. Mix ricotta cheese, ¼ cup Romano cheese, the parsley and egg. Layer noodles, half of the Vegetable Sauce, half of the cheese mixture, the remaining sauce and cheese mixture in baking dish. Cover and bake about 1 hour or until sauce is hot and bubbly. Sprinkle with mozzarella cheese and 2 tablespoons Romano cheese. Bake uncovered 10 to 15 minutes longer or until cheese is hot and bubbly. Let stand about 15 minutes before serving.

VEGETABLE SAUCE

2 small zucchini, cut into fourths

½ green bell pepper, cut into fourths

1 small onion, cut into fourths

3 medium tomatoes, seeded and cut into fourths

1 can (8 ounces) tomato sauce

2 cloves garlic, finely chopped

1 tablespoon chopped fresh or 1 teaspoon dried basil leaves

1 tablespoon chopped fresh or 1 teaspoon dried oregano leaves

1 teaspoon salt

¼ teaspoon fennel seed

Place zucchini, bell pepper and onion in food processor. Cover and process about 10 seconds, using quick on-and-off motions, until mixture is coarsely chopped. Place in 2-quart saucepan. Place tomatoes in food processor. Cover and process about 10 seconds, using quick on-and-off motions, until tomatoes are coarsely chopped. Stir tomatoes into vegetable mixture. Heat to boiling; reduce heat. Simmer uncovered 10 to 12 minutes or until vegetables are tender. Drain well; stir in remaining ingredients.

TRIPLE-CHEESE RAVIOLI

Per Serving			
Calories	170	Fat	4 g (36 calories)
Protein	8 g	Cholesterol	30 mg
Carbohydrate	23 g	Sodium	260 mg

4 Servings, about 1 cup each

1 package (8 ounces) dried cheese-filled ravioli or tortellini

2 cups chopped tomatoes (about 2 large or 1 pound)

½ cup sliced mushrooms (about 1½ ounces)

¼ cup chopped onion (about 1 small)

¼ cup dry red wine or chicken broth

1 tablespoon chopped fresh or 1 teaspoon dried basil leaves

⅛ teaspoon salt

⅛ teaspoon pepper

1 clove garlic, finely chopped

½ cup low-fat ricotta cheese

2 tablespoons grated Parmesan cheese

Cook ravioli as directed on package; drain. Cook remaining ingredients except cheeses in 10-inch skillet over medium-high heat about 5 minutes, stirring frequently, until tomatoes are soft.

Heat oven to 325°. Place ravioli in ungreased square baking dish, 8×8×2 inches. Spread ricotta cheese over ravioli. Pour tomato sauce over top. Sprinkle with Parmesan cheese. Bake uncovered about 20 minutes or until hot.

CHAPTER 5
SATISFYING SOUPS AND STEWS

Spicy Black Bean and Pork Stew (page 94)

CREAMY FISH CHOWDER

This rich-looking chowder is light on calories but full of flavor.

——————— Per Serving ———————			
Calories	225	Fat 2 g (18 calories)	
Protein	19 g	Cholesterol	35 mg
Carbohydrate	32 g	Sodium	1070 mg

8 Servings, about 1 cup each

2 cups cubed potatoes (about 2 medium)

1 cup ¼-inch slices carrots (about 2 medium)

½ cup chopped onion (about 1 medium)

1 cup clam juice

1 cup water

1 tablespoon reduced-calorie margarine

½ teaspoon salt

¼ teaspoon pepper

1 pound haddock or other lean fish fillets, cut into 1-inch pieces

1 can (6½ ounces) whole clams, undrained

1 can (12 ounces) evaporated skim milk

2 tablespoons chopped fresh chives

1 teaspoon paprika

Heat potatoes, carrots, onion, clam juice, water, margarine, salt and pepper to boiling in 3-quart saucepan; reduce heat. Cover and simmer 15 to 20 minutes or until potatoes are almost tender.

Stir in fish and clams. Cover and heat to boiling; reduce heat. Simmer about 5 minutes or until fish flakes easily with fork. Stir in milk, chives and paprika; heat through.

CATFISH STEW

Per Serving			
Calories	225	Fat 6 g (54 calories)	
Protein	17 g	Cholesterol	45 mg
Carbohydrate	27 g	Sodium	270 mg

6 Servings, about 1⅓ cups each

2 medium onions, sliced

1 clove garlic, finely chopped

2 teaspoons chili powder

2 teaspoons vegetable oil

1 can (28 ounces) whole tomatoes, undrained

1¾ cups water

½ cup uncooked regular long grain rice

2 teaspoons chopped fresh or ½ teaspoon dried oregano leaves

2 teaspoons chopped fresh or ½ teaspoon dried thyme leaves

½ teaspoon ground cumin

½ teaspoon red pepper sauce

1 package (10 ounces) frozen sliced okra

1 pound catfish or other medium-fat fish fillets, cut into 1-inch pieces

½ cup chopped green bell pepper (about 1 small)

Cook onions, garlic and chili powder in oil in nonstick Dutch oven over medium heat 2 to 3 minutes, stirring occasionally, until onions are softened. Stir in tomatoes, water, rice, oregano, thyme, cumin and pepper sauce; break up tomatoes. Heat to boiling; reduce heat. Cover and simmer 20 minutes.

Rinse okra with cold water to separate; drain. Stir okra, fish and bell pepper into tomato mixture. Heat to boiling; reduce heat. Cover and simmer 5 to 10 minutes, stirring occasionally, until fish flakes easily with fork and okra is done.

RED SNAPPER STEW

Per Serving

Calories	320	Fat	6 g (54 calories)
Protein	33 g	Cholesterol	40 mg
Carbohydrate	33 g	Sodium	1160 mg

4 Servings, about 2 cups each

1 medium onion, sliced

1 tablespoon reduced-calorie margarine

4 cups chicken broth

1 cup ¼-inch slices carrots (about 2 medium)

½ cup uncooked regular rice

1 tablespoon lemon juice

½ teaspoon salt

¼ teaspoon dried dill weed

1 teaspoon chopped fresh or ¼ teaspoon dried thyme leaves

¼ teaspoon pepper

1 package (10 ounces) frozen baby Brussels sprouts

1½ pounds red snapper or other lean fish fillets, cut into 1-inch pieces

1 cup sliced mushrooms (about 3 ounces)

Cook and stir onion in margarine in Dutch oven over medium heat until onion is tender, about 5 minutes. Stir in broth, carrots, rice, lemon juice, salt, dill weed, thyme and pepper. Heat to boiling; reduce heat. Cover and simmer until rice is tender, about 20 minutes.

Rinse Brussels sprouts under running cold water to separate; drain. Stir into rice mixture. Heat to boiling; reduce heat. Simmer uncovered 5 minutes. Stir in fish and mushrooms; simmer until fish flakes easily with fork, 5 to 8 minutes longer.

Red Snapper and Celery Cabbage Soup

Celery cabbage is known by many names, such as Napa cabbage, Chinese cabbage and Peking cabbage.

———————	Per Serving	———————
Calories	140	Fat 6 g (54 calories)
Protein	17 g	Cholesterol 20 mg
Carbohydrate	4 g	Sodium 1160 mg

4 Servings, about 1½ cups each

- ½ **pound skinless red snapper, sea bass or other lean fish fillets**
- 1 **teaspoon cornstarch**
- 1 **teaspoon finely chopped gingerroot or ¼ teaspoon ground ginger**
- 1 **teaspoon vegetable oil**
- 1 **teaspoon sesame oil**
- ½ **teaspoon salt**
- ½ **teaspoon light soy sauce**
- ⅛ **teaspoon white pepper**
- 8 **ounces celery cabbage**
- 4 **cups chicken broth**
- 1 **teaspoon sesame oil**
- 2 **tablespoons chopped green onions with tops (about 1 medium)**

Cut fish fillets crosswise into ½-inch slices. Toss fish, cornstarch, gingerroot, vegetable oil, 1 teaspoon sesame oil, the salt, soy sauce and white pepper in medium bowl. Cover and refrigerate 30 minutes. Cut celery cabbage into ½-inch slices.

Heat broth to boiling in 3-quart saucepan. Add celery cabbage. Heat to boiling; stir in fish mixture. Heat to boiling; reduce heat to medium. Simmer uncovered 2 minutes; remove from heat. Stir in 1 teaspoon sesame oil and the onions.

SHRIMP GUMBO

You can substitute 3 cups cut-up chicken for the shrimp —calories will increase about 40 per serving.

	Per Serving		
Calories	320	Fat 6 g (54 calories)	
Protein	19 g	Cholesterol	190 mg
Carbohydrate	49 g	Sodium	950 mg

6 Servings, about 1½ cups each

2 tablespoons reduced-calorie margarine

2 medium onions, sliced

1 medium green bell pepper, cut into thin strips

2 cloves garlic, crushed

2 tablespoons all-purpose flour

3 cups beef broth

¼ teaspoon salt

¼ teaspoon pepper

½ teaspoon red pepper sauce

1 bay leaf

1 package (10 ounces) frozen cut okra, thawed, or 1 can (16 ounces) okra, drained

1 can (16 ounces) whole tomatoes, undrained

1 can (6 ounces) tomato paste

1½ pounds fresh or frozen raw medium shrimp (in shells)*

3 cups hot cooked rice

¼ cup chopped fresh parsley

Heat margarine in Dutch oven over medium heat. Cook onions, bell pepper and garlic, stirring occasionally, until onions are softened. Stir in flour. Cook, stirring constantly, until bubbly; remove from heat. Stir in remaining ingredients except shrimp, rice and parsley; break up tomatoes. Heat to boiling; reduce heat. Simmer uncovered 45 minutes, stirring occasionally.

Peel shrimp. (If shrimp are frozen, do not thaw; peel in cold water.) Make a shallow cut lengthwise down back of each shrimp; wash out vein. Stir shrimp into soup. Cover and simmer about 5 minutes or until shrimp are pink. Remove bay leaf. Serve soup over rice and sprinkle with parsley.

*1 pound frozen peeled and deveined raw shrimp, thawed, can be substituted for the 1½ pounds shrimp in shells.

Manhattan Clam Chowder

		Per Serving		
Calories	80	Fat	2 g (18 calories)	
Protein	7 g	Cholesterol	15 mg	
Carbohydrate	10 g	Sodium	540 mg	

4 Servings, about 1½ cups each

- **2 slices thin-sliced bacon, finely chopped**
- **¼ cup chopped onion (about 1 small)**
- **1 pint shucked clams with liquor***
- **2 cups finely chopped potatoes (about 2 medium)**
- **⅓ cup chopped celery**
- **1 cup water**
- **2 teaspoons chopped fresh parsley**
- **½ teaspoon salt**
- **1 teaspoon chopped fresh or ¼ teaspoon dried thyme leaves**
- **⅛ teaspoon pepper**
- **1 can (16 ounces) whole tomatoes, undrained**

Cook bacon and onion in 3-quart saucepan, stirring occasionally, until bacon is crisp and onion is softened. Stir in clams, clam liquor, potatoes, celery and water. Heat to boiling; reduce heat. Cover and simmer about 10 minutes or until potatoes are tender. Stir in remaining ingredients; break up tomatoes. Heat to boiling, stirring occasionally.

*2 cans (6½ ounces each) minced clams, undrained, can be substituted for fresh clams. Stir in clams with remaining ingredients.

Turkey Tortellini Soup

		Per Serving		
Calories	350	Fat	7 g (63 calories)	
Protein	30 g	Cholesterol	60 mg	
Carbohydrate	41 g	Sodium	1070 mg	

4 Servings, about 1½ cups each

- **1 package (7 ounces) dried cheese-filled tortellini**
- **2¼ cups water**
- **2 tablespoons rice wine vinegar or white wine vinegar**
- **2 tablespoons soy sauce**
- **1 can (10¾ ounces) condensed chicken broth**
- **1 to 2 tablespoons finely chopped gingerroot or 1 to 2 teaspoons ground ginger**
- **3 large stalks bok choy with leaves**
- **2 cups cut-up cooked turkey (about 10 ounces)**
- **¼ cup sliced green onions with tops (about 2 medium)**
- **1 cup enoki mushrooms**

Cook tortellini as directed on package; drain. Heat water, vinegar, soy sauce, broth and gingerroot to boiling in 3-quart saucepan; reduce heat.

Separate bok choy leaves from stalks. Cut leaves into thin strips; reserve. Cut stalks into ¼-inch slices. Stir bok choy stalks (reserve leaves), turkey and onions into broth mixture. Simmer uncovered 15 minutes. Stir in bok choy leaves and mushrooms. Simmer just until leaves are wilted.

ORIENTAL BROTH WITH TURKEY

Per Serving			
Calories	235	Fat 8 g (72 calories)	
Protein	22 g	Cholesterol	85 mg
Carbohydrate	10 g	Sodium	660 mg

6 Servings, about 2 cups each

1 pound ground turkey

1 egg

½ cup dry bread crumbs

1½ teaspoons finely chopped ginger-root or ½ teaspoon ground ginger

¼ teaspoon salt

¼ teaspoon pepper

1 teaspoon sesame or vegetable oil

2 large stalks bok choy with leaves

2 cups thinly sliced carrots (about 4 medium)

1 cup dry white wine or chicken broth

2 cans (14½ ounces each) chicken broth

Mix ground turkey, egg, bread crumbs, gingerroot, salt and pepper. Shape into 1-inch balls. Cook in oil in nonstick Dutch oven over medium heat about 10 minutes, turning frequently, until brown.

Separate bok choy leaves from stalks. Cut leaves into thin strips; reserve. Cut stalks into ¼-inch slices. Stir boy choy stalks, carrots, wine and broth into Dutch oven. Heat to boiling; reduce heat. Cover and simmer about 20 minutes or until vegetables are crisp-tender. Stir in bok choy leaves just until wilted.

TURKEY AND WILD RICE SOUP

Per Serving			
Calories	260	Fat 7 g (63 calories)	
Protein	34 g	Cholesterol	105 mg
Carbohydrate	16 g	Sodium	510 mg

6 Servings, about 1½ cups each

½ cup uncooked wild rice

3½ cups water

1 tablespoon chicken bouillon granules

2 turkey drumsticks (about 1½ pounds)

2 medium stalks celery with leaves, sliced

½ cup chopped onion (about 1 medium)

2 bay leaves

1 can (16 ounces) stewed tomatoes

Mix all ingredients in Dutch oven. Heat to boiling; reduce heat. Cover and simmer 50 to 60 minutes or until turkey is done and wild rice is tender.

Remove turkey drumsticks; cool about 5 minutes. Remove skin and bones. Cut turkey into bite-size pieces. Stir turkey into soup. Heat until hot. Remove bay leaves.

SOUTHWEST CHICKEN SOUP

You can substitute marinated or pickled red peppers for the fresh. They are available in many supermarkets in the refrigerated or shelf-stable sections. Be sure to drain the light brine in which they are packaged before using.

	Per Serving		
Calories	215	Fat	3 g (27 calories)
Protein	33 g	Cholesterol	70 mg
Carbohydrate	13 g	Sodium	980 mg

4 Servings, about 1½ cups each

2 large red bell peppers

4 skinless boneless chicken breast halves (about 1 pound)

½ cup chopped onion (about 1 medium)

3 cups chicken broth

2 tablespoons lime juice

1 tablespoon chopped fresh cilantro

½ teaspoon salt

¼ teaspoon pepper

2 cloves garlic, crushed

2 cups cubed jicama

Set oven control to broil. Place bell peppers on rack in broiler pan. Broil with tops about 5 inches from heat, turning occasionally, until skin is blistered and evenly browned (not burned). Remove peppers to brown paper bag and close tightly. Let stand 20 minutes.

Place chicken breasts on rack in broiler pan. Broil with tops 5 to 7 inches from heat about 15 minutes, turning once, until juices of chicken run clear. Cool 10 minutes. Cut into bite-size pieces.

Pare peppers; discard skin. Place peppers and onion in blender or food processor. Cover and blend or process until smooth.

Heat pepper mixture, broth, lime juice, cilantro, salt, pepper and garlic to boiling in 2-quart saucepan; reduce heat. Simmer uncovered 15 minutes, stirring occasionally. Stir in chicken and jicama. Heat until hot.

CHICKEN-CABBAGE SOUP

If you are concerned about sodium and would like to lower your sodium consumption, use low-sodium eight-vegetable juice and bouillon granules.

Per Serving			
Calories	315	Fat 10 g (90 calories)	
Protein	39 g	Cholesterol	110 mg
Carbohydrate	17 g	Sodium	850 mg

6 Servings, about 1½ cups each

5 cups finely chopped cabbage (about 1¼ pounds)

3 cups eight-vegetable juice

2 cups water

2 cups ¼-inch slices carrots (about 4 medium)

1 cup chopped celery (about 2 medium stalks)

1 medium onion, sliced

2 tablespoons chicken bouillon granules

¼ teaspoon pepper

3- to 3½-pound broiler-fryer chicken pieces

½ teaspoon paprika

2 tablespoons reduced-calorie margarine

Heat cabbage, vegetable juice, water, carrots, celery, onion, bouillon granules and pepper to boiling in 4-quart Dutch oven; reduce heat. Cover and simmer 30 minutes.

Remove skin and any excess fat from chicken pieces. Cut each breast half into halves. Sprinkle chicken with paprika. Heat margarine in 10-inch nonstick skillet. Cook chicken 15 to 20 minutes or until light brown on all sides. Add chicken to soup mixture. Heat to boiling; reduce heat. Cover and simmer about 30 minutes or until juices of thickest chicken pieces run clear. Serve chicken pieces in soup bowls; pour soup over chicken.

If YOU LIKE TO EAT OUT, here are a few tips to help cut main dish calories at your favorite restaurants:

▲ Go to restaurants that you know broil, grill or bake foods. Ask how foods are prepared so you can make a low-calorie choice.

▲ Consider ordering an appetizer and a tossed green salad instead of a full meal.

▲ Some restaurants pride themselves on the amount of food they serve, but don't be tempted by the 1-pound steak, the ½-pound hamburger or the half chicken. When ordering meat, choose the smallest size piece of meat. A 3-ounce serving, a portion about the size of a deck of playing cards, is satisfying as well as nutritious.

▲ If portions are large, split your dinner with a friend or take half of it home for another meal.

▲ When ordering pasta, choose an appetizer portion, preferably without cream sauce—tomato sauces usually have fewer calories. Also avoid pesto sauces which are oil-based.

▲ Eat slowly and enjoy your meal fully. Cutting calories doesn't mean cutting out good food!

HAMBURGER MINESTRONE

If you use extra-lean ground beef, you'll save 40 calories per serving. Or try ground turkey, and you'll reduce calories by 95 per serving!

		Per Serving		
Calories	250	Fat	5 g (45 calories)	
Protein	25 g	Cholesterol	55 mg	
Carbohydrate	27 g	Sodium	700 mg	

6 Servings, about 1½ cups each

1 pound ground beef

½ cup chopped onion (about 1 medium)

1 clove garlic, crushed

1¼ cups water

1 cup thin slices celery (about 2 medium stalks)

1 cup sliced zucchini (about 1 small)

1 cup shredded cabbage

½ cup uncooked elbow macaroni or broken spaghetti

2 teaspoons beef bouillon granules

1 teaspoon Italian seasoning

1 can (28 ounces) whole tomatoes, undrained

1 can (8 ounces) kidney beans, undrained

1 can (8 ounces) whole kernel corn, undrained

Cook ground beef, onion and garlic in 4-quart Dutch oven, stirring occasionally, until beef is brown; drain. Stir in remaining ingredients; break up tomatoes.

Heat to boiling; reduce heat. Cover and simmer about 15 minutes, stirring occasionally, until macaroni is tender. Serve with grated Parmesan cheese if desired.

Hungarian Beef Goulash

Goulash gets a special spicy quality from Hungarian paprika, considered by many to be the superior variety. Paprika is a powder made by grinding sweet pepper pods, and its flavor ranges from mild to pungent, its color from orange-red to deep red. You'll find the more pungent varieties in markets that stack imported foods.

Per Serving			
Calories	270	Fat	8 g (72 calories)
Protein	27 g	Cholesterol	70 mg
Carbohydrate	22 g	Sodium	920 mg

6 Servings, about 1½ cups each

1 tablespoon vegetable oil

1½ pounds beef boneless chuck, tip or round, cut into ¾-inch cubes

2 cups water

1 can (8 ounces) whole tomatoes, undrained

3 cups chopped onions (about 3 large)

1 clove garlic, chopped

1 tablespoon paprika

2 teaspoons salt

1 teaspoon beef bouillon granules

½ teaspoon caraway seed

¼ teaspoon pepper

2 medium potatoes, cut into 1½-inch pieces

2 green bell peppers, cut into 1-inch pieces

Heat oil in Dutch oven or 12-inch skillet. Cook beef about 15 minutes, stirring occasionally, until brown; drain. Stir in remaining ingredients except potatoes and bell peppers; break up tomatoes. Heat to boiling, reduce heat. Cover and simmer 1 hour.

Stir in potatoes. Cover and simmer about 30 minutes or until beef and potatoes are tender. Stir in bell peppers. Cover and simmer 8 to 10 minutes or until tender. Serve in soup bowls with French bread for dipping into hot broth if desired.

If YOU WANT LESS SODIUM in your soups and stews, the following is a comparison of salt and the various chicken-broth ingredient choices you have from the supermarket and your cupboard shelves:

Ingredient	Milligrams of sodium
1 teaspoon salt	2130
½ teaspoon salt	1065
¼ teaspoon salt	535
1 teaspoon (or 1 cube) chicken bouillon	900
1 teaspoon low-sodium chicken bouillon granules	5
8 ounces prepared condensed canned chicken broth	750
7¼ ounces ready-to-eat canned chicken broth	910
7¼ ounces ready-to-eat canned ⅓ less salt chicken broth	580
10½ ounces ready-to-eat canned low-sodium chicken broth	70

BEEF-VEGETABLE STEW WITH BARLEY

Per Serving			
Calories	290	Fat 9 g (81 calories)	
Protein	23 g	Cholesterol	55 mg
Carbohydrate	23 g	Sodium	330 mg

4 Servings, about 1½ cups each

- **1 pound beef stew meat, cut into 1-inch pieces**
- **1 tablespoon vegetable oil**
- **1 cup dry red wine or beef broth**
- **1 teaspoon chopped fresh or ¼ teaspoon dried rosemary leaves, crushed**
- **¼ teaspoon pepper**
- **1 clove garlic, finely chopped**
- **1 can (10½ ounces) condensed beef broth**
- **1 can (14½ ounces) whole tomatoes, undrained**
- **½ cup uncooked barley**
- **1 cup broccoli flowerets**
- **2 cups sliced carrots (about 2 medium)**
- **1 medium onion, cut into wedges**
- **4 ounces medium mushrooms, cut into halves**

Cook beef in oil in 4-quart Dutch oven, stirring occasionally, until brown. Stir in wine, rosemary, pepper, garlic, broth and tomatoes; break up tomatoes. Heat to boiling; reduce heat. Cover and simmer 1 hour.

Stir in barley. Cover and simmer about 30 minutes or until beef is almost tender. Stir in remaining ingredients. Cover and simmer about 20 minutes or until vegetables are tender.

Spicy Black Bean and Pork Stew

Per Serving			
Calories	340	Fat 11 g (99 calories)	
Protein	26 g	Cholesterol	70 mg
Carbohydrate	30 g	Sodium	340 mg

4 Servings, about 1⅓ cups each

4 cups water

½ cup dried black beans (about 4 ounces)

2 ancho chilies

¾ pound lean pork boneless shoulder

1½ cups chopped peeled tomatoes (about 2 medium)

½ cup chopped onion (about 1 medium)

½ cup dry red wine

1 tablespoon chopped fresh or 1 teaspoon dried sage leaves

1 tablespoon chopped fresh or 1 teaspoon dried marjoram leaves

½ teaspoon salt

½ teaspoon ground cumin

¼ teaspoon ground cinnamon

1 clove garlic, finely chopped

2 cups 1-inch cubes pared butternut squash

1 medium red bell pepper, cut into 1-inch pieces

2 tablespoons chopped fresh cilantro

Heat water, beans and chilies to boiling in 4-quart nonstick Dutch oven. Boil uncovered 2 minutes; remove from heat. Cover and let stand 1 hour. Remove chilies; reserve. Heat beans to boiling; reduce heat. Cover and simmer 1 hour.

Seed and coarsely chop chilies. Trim fat from pork shoulder. Cut pork into 1-inch cubes. Stir pork, chilies and remaining ingredients except squash, bell pepper and cilantro into beans. Heat to boiling; reduce heat. Cover and simmer 30 minutes, stirring occasionally. Stir in squash. Cover and simmer 30 minutes, stirring occasionally, until squash is tender. Stir in bell pepper and cilantro. Cover and simmer about 5 minutes or until bell pepper is crisp-tender.

COUSCOUS SOUP WITH SAUSAGE

Per Serving			
Calories	200	Fat 11 g (99 calories)	
Protein	10 g	Cholesterol	25 mg
Carbohydrate	15 g	Sodium	760 mg

6 Servings, about 1¼ cups each

1 tablespoon chopped jalapeño chilies

½ teaspoon ground cumin

2 cloves garlic, crushed

1 pound fully cooked smoked sausage, cut crosswise into ¼-inch slices

2½ cups water

1 can (10¾ ounces) condensed chicken broth

½ cup couscous

2 tablespoons chopped fresh or 2 teaspoons dried mint leaves

¼ teaspoon pepper

¾ cup chopped tomato (about 1 medium)

Cook chilies, cumin, garlic and sausage in 3-quart saucepan over medium heat about 8 minutes or until sausage is brown; drain.

Add water and broth. Heat to boiling. Stir in couscous, mint and pepper; reduce heat. Cover and simmer 5 minutes. Stir in tomato. Serve with chopped fresh parsley and finely chopped garlic if desired.

LENTIL VEGETABLE SOUP

Per Serving			
Calories	165	Fat	1 g (9 calories)
Protein	11 g	Cholesterol	0 mg
Carbohydrate	32 g	Sodium	590 mg

6 Servings, about 1½ cups each

1 cup chopped onion (about 1 large)

2 teaspoons chili powder

1 teaspoon salt

1 teaspoon ground cumin

2 cloves garlic, finely chopped

1 can (6 ounces) spicy tomato juice

3 cups water

1 cup dried lentils, sorted and rinsed (about 6 ounces)

1 can (14½ ounces) whole tomatoes, undrained

1 can (4 ounces) chopped green chilies, undrained

1 cup fresh or frozen whole kernel corn

2 cups julienne strips zucchini (about 2 small)

Heat onion, chili powder, salt, cumin, garlic and tomato juice to boiling in 3-quart saucepan; reduce heat. Cover and simmer 5 minutes. Stir in remaining ingredients except corn and zucchini. Heat to boiling; reduce heat. Cover and simmer 20 minutes. Stir in corn; cover and simmer 10 minutes. Stir in zucchini; cover and simmer about 5 minutes or until lentils and zucchini are tender.

Cuban Black Bean Soup

Black beans, also called "turtle beans," have black skin, cream-colored flesh and a sweet flavor. They are popular in the Caribbean, Central and South America, Mexico and the southern United States.

--- Per Serving ---

Calories	295	Fat	6 g (54 calories)
Protein	18 g	Cholesterol	5 mg
Carbohydrate	40 g	Sodium	510 mg

8 Servings, about 1¼ cups each

1 cup chopped onion (about 1 large)

3 cloves garlic, finely chopped

2 tablespoons vegetable oil

1 pound dried black beans (about 2⅔ cups)

3 cups beef broth

3 cups water

1 cup finely chopped fully cooked smoked extra-lean ham

1 cup chopped green bell pepper

1 cup chopped tomato (about 1 large)

¼ cup dark rum

1½ teaspoons ground cumin

1 tablespoon chopped fresh or 1½ teaspoons dried oregano leaves

Cook onion and the garlic in oil in Dutch oven, stirring occasionally, until onion is softened. Stir in remaining ingredients. Heat to boiling. Boil 2 minutes; reduce heat. Cover and simmer about 2 hours or until beans are tender. Serve with chopped hard-cooked egg and chopped onion if desired.

Hearty Bean and Pasta Stew

--- Per Serving ---

Calories	350	Fat	4 g (36 calories)
Protein	20 g	Cholesterol	0 mg
Carbohydrate	59 g	Sodium	690 mg

4 Servings, about 1 cup each

1 cup coarsely chopped tomato (about 1 large)

¾ cup uncooked shell macaroni

¼ cup chopped onion (about 1 small)

¼ cup chopped green bell pepper (about ½ small)

1 tablespoon chopped fresh or 1 teaspoon dried basil leaves

1 teaspoon Worcestershire sauce

1 clove garlic, finely chopped

1 can (16 ounces) kidney beans, drained

1 can (8 ounces) garbanzo beans, drained

1 can (14½ ounces) chicken broth

Mix all ingredients in 2-quart saucepan. Heat to boiling, stirring occasionally; reduce heat. Cover and simmer about 15 minutes, stirring occasionally, until macaroni is tender.

ZUCCHINI SOUP

Zucchini, low in calories, is a plentiful plant for home gardeners, as well as readily available year 'round.

	Per Serving		
Calories	205	Fat 10 g (90 calories)	
Protein	10 g	Cholesterol	20 mg
Carbohydrate	19 g	Sodium	820 mg

4 Servings, about 1½ cups each

¼ cup chopped onion (about 1 small)

1 tablespoon reduced-calorie margarine

2 cups chicken broth

2 tablespoons finely chopped canned green chilies

½ teaspoon salt

⅛ teaspoon pepper

2 cups chopped zucchini (about 2 small)

1 can (8¾ ounces) whole kernel corn, drained

1 cup milk

2 ounces Monterey Jack cheese, cut into ¼-inch cubes (½ cup)

Ground nutmeg

Chopped fresh parsley

Cook onion in margarine in 2-quart saucepan, stirring occasionally, until onion is softened. Stir in broth, chilies, salt, pepper, zucchini and corn. Heat to boiling; reduce heat. Cover and simmer about 5 minutes or until zucchini is tender. Stir in milk; heat until hot. Stir in cheese. Garnish with nutmeg and parsley.

SPICY VEGETABLE STEW

―――――――	Per Serving	―――――――
Calories	210	Fat 7 g (63 calories)
Protein	9 g	Cholesterol 0 mg
Carbohydrate	32 g	Sodium 890 mg

6 Servings, about 1⅓ cups each

¾ cup chopped onion

1 clove garlic, finely chopped

2 tablespoons vegetable oil

1 large red bell pepper, cut into 2 × ½-inch strips

2 medium poblano or Anaheim chilies, seeded and cut into 2 × ½-inch strips

1 jalapeño chili, seeded and chopped

1 cup cubed Hubbard or acorn squash (about ½ pound)

2 cans (14½ ounces each) chicken broth

½ teaspoon salt

½ teaspoon pepper

½ teaspoon ground coriander

1 cup thinly sliced zucchini (about 1 small)

1 cup thinly sliced yellow squash (about 1 small)

1 can (17 ounces) whole kernel corn, drained

1 can (16 ounces) pinto beans, drained

Cook onion and garlic in oil in Dutch oven over medium heat, stirring occasionally, until onion is softened. Stir in bell pepper, poblano and jalapeño chilies. Cook 15 minutes, stirring occasionally.

Stir in Hubbard squash, broth, salt, pepper and coriander. Heat to boiling; reduce heat. Cover and simmer about 15 minutes or until squash is tender. Stir in remaining ingredients. Cook uncovered about 10 minutes, stirring occasionally, until zucchini is tender.

ITALIAN VEGETABLE SOUP

Per Serving			
Calories	195	Fat	4 g (36 calories)
Protein	13 g	Cholesterol	5 mg
Carbohydrate	29 g	Sodium	1170 mg

4 Servings, about 1½ cups each

½ cup dried great northern, navy or kidney beans (about 4 ounces)

1 cup water

4 cups chicken broth

2 small tomatoes, chopped (about 1 cup)

2 medium carrots, sliced (about 1 cup)

1 stalk celery, sliced (about ½ cup)

1 medium onion, chopped (about ½ cup)

1 clove garlic, chopped

½ cup uncooked macaroni

1 tablespoon chopped fresh parsley

½ teaspoon salt

1½ teaspoons chopped fresh or ½ teaspoon dried basil

⅛ teaspoon pepper

1 bay leaf

¾ cup cut green beans

2 small zucchini, cut into 1-inch slices (about 2 cups)

Grated Parmesan cheese

Heat dried beans and water to boiling in Dutch oven. Boil uncovered 2 minutes; remove from heat. Cover and let stand 1 hour. (Add enough water to cover beans if necessary.) Heat to boiling; reduce heat. Cover and simmer 1 to 1½ hours or until tender.

Add chicken broth, tomatoes, carrots, celery, onion, garlic, macaroni, parsley, salt, basil, pepper and bay leaf to beans. Heat to boiling; reduce heat. Cover and simmer 15 minutes. Add green beans and zucchini. Heat to boiling; reduce heat. Cover and simmer 10 to 15 minutes or until macaroni and vegetables are tender. Remove bay leaf. Serve soup with cheese.

CHAPTER 6
FILLING MEATLESS MAINSTAYS

Herbed Eggs and Vegetables on Polenta (page 106)

Eggs Benedict

This Mock Hollandaise Sauce is a satisfying substitute for the traditional rich sauce. It's also delicious on vegetables!

———————	Per Serving	———————
Calories	225	Fat 13 g (117 calories)
Protein	14 g	Cholesterol 285 mg
Carbohydrate	11 g	Sodium 720 mg

4 Servings

Mock Hollandaise Sauce (right)

4 thin slices Canadian-style bacon (about 2 ounces)

4 Poached Eggs (right)

2 English muffins, split and toasted

Prepare Mock Hollandaise Sauce; keep warm. Spray 10-inch nonstick skillet with nonstick cooking spray. Cook bacon in skillet over medium heat until light brown on both sides.

Prepare Poached Eggs. Place 1 slice bacon on split side of each muffin half; top with egg. Spoon ¼ of the warm sauce (about 3 tablespoons) onto each egg.

Mock Hollandaise Sauce

2 tablespoons reduced-calorie margarine

1 tablespoon all-purpose flour

¼ teaspoon salt

⅔ cup skim milk

1 egg yolk

½ teaspoon grated lemon peel

2 teaspoons lemon juice

Heat margarine in 1-quart nonstick saucepan over low heat until melted. Stir in flour and salt. Cook over low heat, stirring constantly, until mixture is smooth and bubbly; remove from heat. Mix milk and egg yolk until smooth; stir into flour mixture. Heat to boiling, stirring constantly. Boil and stir 1 minute; remove from heat. Stir in lemon peel and lemon juice.

Poached Eggs

Heat water (1½ to 2 inches) to boiling; reduce to simmering. Break each egg into custard cup or saucer. Hold cup close to water's surface and slip 1 egg at a time into water. Cook 3 to 5 minutes or until of desired doneness. Remove eggs from water with slotted spoon.

VEGETABLE-FILLED SOUFFLE ROLL

To seed tomatoes, cut in half crosswise and squeeze gently—seeds are easily and quickly released.

	Per Serving		
Calories	310	Fat 19 g (171 calories)	
Protein	15 g	Cholesterol	240 mg
Carbohydrate	18 g	Sodium	590 mg

4 Servings, 2 slices (¾ inch thick) each

¼ cup reduced-calorie margarine

¼ cup all-purpose flour

½ teaspoon salt

Dash of ground red pepper (cayenne)

1½ cups skim milk

4 egg yolks

6 egg whites

½ teaspoon cream of tartar

Basil Vegetables (right)

Spray bottom of jelly roll pan, 15½ × 10½ × 1 inch, with nonstick cooking spray. Line bottom of pan with waxed paper; spray with nonstick cooking spray. Heat margarine in 2-quart saucepan over low heat until melted. Stir in flour, salt and red pepper. Cook, stirring constantly, until smooth and bubbly; remove from heat. Stir in milk. Heat to boiling, stirring constantly. Boil and stir 1 minute; remove from heat. Beat in egg yolks, one at a time.

Heat oven to 350°. Beat egg whites and cream of tartar in large bowl on high speed until stiff but not dry. Stir about one-fourth of the egg whites into egg yolk mixture. Fold egg yolk mixture into remaining egg whites. Spread evenly in pan. Bake uncovered 35 to 40 minutes or until puffed and golden brown.

While soufflé is baking, prepare Basil Vegetables. Immediately loosen soufflé from edges of pan; invert onto cloth-covered wire rack. Carefully peel off waxed paper. Spread soufflé with Basil Vegetables; roll up from narrow end. Serve immediately.

BASIL VEGETABLES

¼ cup chopped onion (about 1 small)

2 large cloves garlic, finely chopped

1 tablespoon olive or vegetable oil

2 cups chopped seeded tomatoes (about 2 large)

1½ cups thinly sliced zucchini (about 1 small)

¼ cup chopped fresh or 1 tablespoon dried basil leaves

¼ cup grated Parmesan cheese

Cook onion and garlic in oil in 10-inch nonstick skillet over medium-high heat about 2 minutes, stirring occasionally, until onion is tender. Stir in tomatoes, zucchini and basil. Heat to boiling; reduce heat. Simmer uncovered about 3 minutes or until zucchini is crisp-tender. Stir in cheese.

Herbed Eggs and Vegetables on Polenta

Polenta, a staple in northern Italy and eastern European countries, is a type of cornmeal pudding. It is also popular cooled, then sliced and fried or baked and served with other foods.

———————	Per Serving	———————
Calories	170	Fat 4 g (36 calories)
Protein	6 g	Cholesterol 55 mg
Carbohydrate	28 g	Sodium 680 mg

4 Servings, about ½ cup polenta
and ¾ cup egg mixture each

⅔ cup yellow cornmeal

½ cup cold water

2 cups boiling water

1 tablespoon chopped fresh or 1 teaspoon dried basil leaves

½ teaspoon salt

1 tablespoon reduced-calorie margarine

8 ounces small whole mushrooms

1 medium onion, sliced

1 medium red bell pepper, cut into strips

1 tablespoon chopped fresh or 1 teaspoon dried basil leaves

½ cup chicken broth

2 teaspoons cornstarch

½ teaspoon salt

6 hard-cooked eggs, cut lengthwise into halves

Mix cornmeal and cold water in 2-quart nonstick saucepan. Stir in boiling water, 1 tablespoon basil and ½ teaspoon salt. Cook, stirring occasionally, until mixture thickens and boils; reduce heat to low. Cook about 10 minutes, stirring occasionally, until very thick; remove from heat. Keep warm.

Heat margarine in 10-inch nonstick skillet over medium heat. Cook mushrooms, onion, bell pepper and 1 tablespoon basil about 7 minutes, stirring occasionally, until onion is softened. Stir broth into cornstarch and ½ teaspoon salt. Stir into vegetable mixture. Heat to boiling, stirring occasionally. Boil and stir 1 minute; reduce heat.

Carefully stir eggs into vegetable mixture. Simmer uncovered 3 to 5 minutes, without stirring, until eggs are hot. Serve over polenta.

If YOU LIKE EGGS, but are concerned about cholesterol and reluctant to eat them, try using an egg substitute. Several brands are readily available in the frozen or refrigerated sections of your supermarket. Or, make your own.

One large egg equals about ¼ cup. Substitute the ½ cup recipe below for 2 whole eggs or ½ cup cholesterol-free egg product. For even color, mix egg white and food color well before adding oil.

For ½ cup: 3 egg whites
              3 drops yellow food color
              1 teaspoon vegetable oil

For 1 cup: 6 egg whites
             6 drops yellow food color
             2 teaspoons vegetable oil

Mix egg whites and food color. Mix in oil. Cover and refrigerate no longer than 2 days. 2 or 4 servings, about ¼ cup each.

Per serving for 1 egg:

Calories	80	Fat	6 g (54 calories)
Protein	6 g	Cholesterol	275 mg
Carbohydrate	1 g	Sodium	70 mg

Per serving for egg substitute:

Calories	45	Fat	2 g (18 calories)
Protein	5 g	Cholesterol	0 mg
Carbohydrate	1 g	Sodium	80 mg

ONION OMELET WITH TOMATOES

	Per Serving		
Calories	190	Fat	11 g (99 calories)
Protein	10 g	Cholesterol	215 mg
Carbohydrate	14 g	Sodium	240 mg

4 Servings

1 tablespoon olive or vegetable oil

2 large onions, sliced

2 tablespoons chopped walnuts

4 eggs, separated

2 egg whites

¼ cup water

¼ teaspoon salt

2 cups chopped tomatoes (about 2 large)

Heat oven to 325°. Heat oil in 10-inch nonstick ovenproof skillet over medium heat. Cook onions in oil about 5 minutes, stirring frequently, until onions are light golden brown. Stir in walnuts.

Beat 6 egg whites, water and salt in large bowl on high speed until stiff but not dry. Beat 4 egg yolks on high speed about 3 minutes or until very thick and lemon colored. Fold into egg white mixture. Pour into skillet. Level surface gently; reduce heat to low. Cook about 5 minutes or until puffed and light brown on bottom. (Lift omelet carefully at edge to judge color.) Bake uncovered in oven 12 to 15 minutes or until knife inserted in center comes out clean. Tilt skillet; slip pancake turner or spatula under omelet to loosen. Invert onto warm platter; cut into wedges. Serve with chopped tomatoes.

WINTER SQUASH SOUFFLE

Per Serving			
Calories	195	Fat	9 g (81 calories)
Protein	11 g	Cholesterol	165 mg
Carbohydrate	17 g	Sodium	330 mg

4 Servings

¼ **cup chopped onion (about 1 small)**

2 **tablespoons reduced-calorie margarine**

2 **tablespoons all-purpose flour**

¼ **teaspoon salt**

¼ **teaspoon ground nutmeg**

⅛ **teaspoon pepper**

1 **cup skim milk**

3 **eggs, separated**

1 **package (12 ounces) frozen squash, thawed**

2 **egg whites**

½ **teaspoon cream of tartar**

2 **tablespoons grated Parmesan cheese**

Heat oven to 350°. Make a 4-inch band of triple-thickness aluminum foil 2 inches longer than circumference of 6-cup soufflé dish or 1½-quart casserole; secure foil band around top edge of dish. Spray inside of dish and foil with nonstick cooking spray.

Cook onion in margarine in 2-quart non-stick saucepan until onion is softened. Stir in flour, salt, nutmeg and pepper. Cook over low heat, stirring constantly, until margarine is absorbed; remove from heat. Beat milk and egg yolks; stir into flour mixture. Heat to boiling, stirring constantly. Boil and stir 1 minute. Stir in squash.

Beat egg whites and cream of tartar in medium bowl on high speed until stiff but not dry. Stir about one-fourth of the egg white mixture into squash mixture. Fold squash mixture into remaining egg white mixture.

Carefully pour into soufflé dish. Bake uncovered about 50 minutes or until set and cracks feel dry when touched lightly. Carefully remove foil band and divide soufflé into 4 servings with 2 forks. Sprinkle each serving with Parmesan cheese. Serve immediately.

EGGS AND SPINACH CASSEROLE

	Per Serving		
Calories	255	Fat 12 g (108 calories)	
Protein	12 g	Cholesterol	230 mg
Carbohydrate	24 g	Sodium	320 mg

6 Servings

- **½ cup chopped onion (about 1 medium)**
- **1 tablespoon reduced-calorie margarine**
- **3 cups frozen shredded hash brown potatoes**
- **½ teaspoon herb seasoning mix**
- **½ teaspoon salt**
- **1 package (10 ounces) frozen chopped spinach, thawed**
- **½ cup shredded low-fat Swiss cheese (2 ounces)**
- **½ cup low-fat sour cream**
- **6 eggs**

Heat oven to 350°. Cook onion in margarine in 10-inch skillet over medium heat until softened, stirring occasionally. Stir in frozen potatoes, seasoning mix, salt and spinach. Cook about 3 minutes, stirring constantly, just until potatoes are thawed. Stir in cheese and sour cream. Spread in ungreased square baking dish, 8 × 8 × 2 inches.

Make 6 indentations in potato mixture with back of spoon; break 1 egg into each indentation. Sprinkle with pepper if desired.

Bake uncovered 30 to 35 minutes or until eggs are of desired doneness.

CHILAQUILES CASSEROLE

	Per Serving		
Calories	295	Fat 15 g (135 calories)	
Protein	15 g	Cholesterol	45 mg
Carbohydrate	26 g	Sodium	1070 mg

6 Servings, about 1 cup each

- **4 flour tortillas (about 8 inches in diameter), cut into ½-inch strips**
- **1 can (16 ounces) pinto beans, drained**
- **1 bottle (16 ounces) red or green salsa (about 1¾ cups)**
- **2 cups shredded Monterey Jack cheese (8 ounces)**
- **⅓ cup low-fat sour cream**
- **⅓ cup plain nonfat yogurt**
- **1 tablespoon chopped fresh cilantro or parsley**

Heat oven to 350°. Spray 2-quart casserole with nonstick cooking spray. Layer half of the tortilla strips in bottom of casserole. Top with beans, half of the salsa and 1 cup of the cheese. Repeat with remaining tortilla strips, salsa and cheese. Bake uncovered about 30 minutes or until cheese is melted and golden brown.

Mix sour cream, yogurt and cilantro. Top each serving with about 2 tablespoons sour cream mixture.

GRUYERE PUFF IN MUSHROOM CRUST

Our unusual mushroom crust helps keep this innovative main dish at about 200 calories per serving.

	Per Serving		
Calories	220	Fat 14 g (126 calories)	
Protein	12 g	Cholesterol	95 mg
Carbohydrate	12 g	Sodium	210 mg

6 Servings

Mushroom Crust (right)

1 small onion, sliced

2 tablespoons reduced-calorie margarine

2 tablespoons all-purpose flour

¼ teaspoon dry mustard

1 cup skim milk

1 cup shredded Gruyère cheese (4 ounces)

2 eggs, separated

1 egg white

1 tablespoon chopped fresh chives

Prepare Mushroom Crust. Reduce oven temperature to 350°. Cook onion in margarine in 1-quart nonstick saucepan over low heat about 3 minutes or until onion is softened. Stir in flour and mustard until blended; remove from heat. Stir in milk. Heat to boiling over low heat, stirring constantly. Boil and stir 1 minute; remove from heat. Stir in cheese until melted.

Beat egg whites in medium bowl until stiff but not dry. Beat egg yolks until light and lemon colored. Stir egg yolks into cheese mixture. Stir about one-fourth of the egg whites into cheese mixture. Fold cheese mixture into remaining egg whites; stir in chives. Spread in Mushroom Crust. Bake uncovered about 30 minutes or until golden brown and cracks feel dry.

MUSHROOM CRUST

3 cups finely chopped mushrooms (about 12 ounces)

1 large clove garlic, finely chopped

2 tablespoons reduced-calorie margarine

¼ cup dry bread crumbs

1 egg white

Heat oven to 375°. Spray pie plate, 9 × 1¼ inches, with nonstick cooking spray. Cook mushrooms and garlic in margarine in 10-inch nonstick skillet over medium heat about 5 minutes or until most of the moisture is evaporated; cool slightly. Stir in bread crumbs. Beat egg white until stiff peaks form; stir into mushroom mixture. Spread in pie plate. Bake about 10 minutes or until edge begins to brown and crust is set.

THREE-CHEESE PIE

—————— Per Serving ——————

Calories	225	Fat 15 g (135 calories)	
Protein	15 g	Cholesterol	145 mg
Carbohydrate	7 g	Sodium	430 mg

8 Servings

1 cup shredded Cheddar cheese (4 ounces)

1 cup shredded mozzarella cheese (4 ounces)

1 cup shredded Monterey Jack cheese (4 ounces)

½ cup chopped onion (about 1 medium)

2 tablespoons all-purpose flour

4 eggs

1 cup skim milk

½ teaspoon salt

½ teaspoon dry msutard

½ teaspoon Worcestershire sauce

2 medium tomatoes, sliced

Heat oven to 350°. Grease pie plate, 10 × 1½ inches, or quiche dish, 9 × 1½ inches. Mix cheeses, onion and flour. Spread in pie plate. Beat eggs slightly in large bowl. Beat in milk, salt, mustard and Worcestershire sauce. Pour over cheese mixture. Bake uncovered 35 to 40 minutes or until set. Let stand 10 minutes. Arrange tomato slices, overlapping slightly, around edge of pie.

GREEK OVEN PANCAKE

—————— Per Serving ——————

Calories	255	Fat 16 g (144 calories)	
Protein	11 g	Cholesterol	140 mg
Carbohydrate	15 g	Sodium	650 mg

4 Servings

2 tablespoons reduced-calorie margarine

½ cup all-purpose flour

½ cup skim milk

¼ teaspoon Italian seasoning

¼ teaspoon salt

2 eggs

1 teaspoon reduced-calorie margarine

1 cup julienne strips zucchini (about 1 small)

1 cup crumbled feta cheese (5 ounces)

2 tablespoons chopped Greek olives

Heat oven to 425°. Heat 2 tablespoons margarine in square pan, 9 × 9 × 2 inches, in oven about 4 minutes or until hot and bubbly. Beat flour, milk, Italian seasoning, salt and eggs with hand beater until well blended. Pour into pan. Bake uncovered 20 to 25 minutes or until sides of pancake are puffed and deep golden brown.

Heat 1 teaspoon margarine in 1½-quart nonstick saucepan over medium heat. Cook zucchini about 2 minutes, stirring frequently, until crisp-tender. Carefully stir in cheese. Spoon onto center of pancake; sprinkle with olives.

SPICY BLACK BEAN BURRITOS

By using evaporated skim milk rather than regular skim milk, you'll make a sauce that's thicker and whiter.

——————— Per Serving ———————			
Calories	265	Fat	8 g (72 calories)
Protein	13 g	Cholesterol	0 mg
Carbohydrate	37 g	Sodium	180 mg

6 Servings

Pumpkin Seed Sauce (right)

1 cup chopped broccoli

½ cup chopped onion (about 1 medium)

2 cloves garlic, finely chopped

1 tablespoon reduced-calorie margarine

1 can (15 ounces) black beans, drained

1 cup julienne strips yellow squash (about 1 medium)

1 small red bell pepper, cut into 2 × ¼-inch strips

2 tablespoons shelled pumpkin seeds, toasted

1 tablespoon lemon juice

¼ teaspoon red pepper flakes

¼ teaspoon ground cumin

6 flour tortillas (about 8 inches in diameter), warmed

Prepare Pumpkin Seed Sauce; keep warm. Cook broccoli, onion and garlic in margarine in 10-inch nonstick skillet, stirring frequently, until onion is softened. Stir in remaining ingredients except tortillas. Cook uncovered, stirring occasionally, until squash and bell pepper are crisp-tender.

Spoon about ½ cup of the vegetable mixture onto center of each tortilla. Fold one end of tortilla up about 1 inch over mixture; fold right and left sides over, overlapping. Fold remaining end down. Serve with Pumpkin Seed Sauce.

PUMPKIN SEED SAUCE

1 tablespoon reduced-calorie margarine

2 tablespoons chopped onion

1 small clove garlic, crushed

2 tablespoons shelled pumpkin seeds

1 slice whole wheat bread, torn into small pieces

1 tablespoon canned chopped green chilies

¼ cup chicken broth

¼ cup evaporated skim milk

Dash of salt

Cook onion and garlic in margarine, stirring frequently, until onion is softened. Stir in pumpkin seeds and bread. Cook over medium heat, stirring frequently, until bread is golden brown. Stir in chilies. Place mixture in blender or food processor. Cover and blend or process until finely ground. Add broth, milk and salt. Cover and process until blended.

BEAN-CHEESE PIE

Per Serving			
Calories	315	Fat 11 g (99 calories)	
Protein	18 g	Cholesterol	50 mg
Carbohydrate	40 g	Sodium	730 mg

8 Servings

¾ cup all-purpose flour

½ cup shredded Cheddar cheese (2 ounces)

1½ teaspoons baking powder

½ teaspoon salt

⅓ cup milk

1 egg, slightly beaten

1 can (15½ ounces) garbanzo beans, drained

1 can (15 ounces) kidney beans, drained

1 can (8 ounces) tomato sauce

½ cup chopped green bell pepper (about 1 small)

¼ cup chopped onion (about 1 small)

2 teaspoons chili powder

2 teaspoons fresh or ½ teaspoon dried oregano leaves

¼ teaspoon garlic powder

½ cup shredded Cheddar cheese (2 ounces)

Heat oven to 375°. Spray pie plate, 10 × 1½ inches, with nonstick cooking spray. Mix flour, ½ cup cheese, the baking powder and salt in medium bowl. Stir in milk and egg until blended. Spread over bottom and up side of pie plate. Mix remaining ingredients except ½ cup cheese. Spoon into pie plate; sprinkle with ½ cup cheese. Bake uncovered about 25 minutes or until edge is puffy and light brown. Let stand 10 minutes before cutting.

If YOU LIKE CHEESE, substitute the light or reduced fat counterpart for your favorite regular hard cheeses or choose lower calorie cheeses. The following calorie chart shows the calories in 1 ounce of cheese:

American	105
American, light	70
Cheddar	115
Cheddar, light	50
Cream cheese	100
Cream cheese (light or Neuchatel)	75
Monterey Jack	110
Monterey Jack, light	80
Mozzarella, whole milk	80
Mozzarella, part-skim	70
Swiss	105
Swiss, light	70

BEAN-STUFFED CABBAGE ROLLS

For variety, try different types of beans, such as pinto, kidney or black beans.

———————	Per Serving	———————	
Calories	175	Fat	3 g (27 calories)
Protein	8 g	Cholesterol	0 mg
Carbohydrate	32 g	Sodium	440 mg

6 Servings, 2 rolls each

1 large head cabbage (about 3 pounds)

1 tablespoon reduced-calorie margarine

¼ cup chopped onion (about 1 small)

2 teaspoons chopped fresh or ½ teaspoon dried sage leaves

¼ teaspoon ground cumin

1 clove garlic, finely chopped

1½ cups finely shredded cabbage

½ cup shredded carrot (about 1 medium)

1 can (19 ounces) cannellini beans, drained

½ cup chicken broth

½ cup skim milk

2 teaspoons cornstarch

1 teaspoon chopped fresh or ¼ teaspoon dried sage leaves

¼ teaspoon salt

6 tablespoons shredded low-fat Swiss cheese

Remove core from cabbage. Cover cabbage with warm water; let stand about 10 minutes or until leaves loosen slightly. Remove 12 cabbage leaves. Cover leaves with boiling water. Cover and let stand about 10 minutes or until leaves are limp; drain.

Heat oven to 350°. Heat margarine in 2-quart nonstick saucepan over medium heat. Cook onion, 2 teaspoons chopped fresh sage, the cumin and garlic about 3 minutes, stirring frequently, until onion is softened. Stir in shredded cabbage, carrot and beans.

Place scant ¼ cup bean mixture at stem end of cabbage leaf. Roll leaf around bean mixture, tucking in sides. Place cabbage rolls, seam sides down, in ungreased rectangular baking dish, 13 × 9 × 2 inches. Pour broth over rolls. Cover and bake 30 to 35 minutes or until rolls are hot.

Remove cabbage rolls with slotted spoon; keep warm. Drain liquid from baking dish, reserving ½ cup. Gradually stir milk into cornstarch in saucepan until smooth; stir in reserved liquid, 1 teaspoon chopped fresh sage and the salt. Heat to boiling over medium heat, stirring constantly. Boil and stir 1 minute. Serve sauce over cabbage rolls; sprinkle each serving with 1 tablespoon cheese.

Whole Stuffed Pumpkin (page 120)
Spicy Black Bean Burritos (page 113)

Whole Stuffed Pumpkin

A stunning dish, sure to appeal to anyone with an interest in the unusual! Make this in an attractive ovenproof pie plate or baking dish for the most striking presentation.

———	Per Serving	———
Calories	215	Fat	4 g (36 calories)
Protein	6 g	Cholesterol	0 mg
Carbohydrate	44 g	Sodium	450 mg

6 Servings

- **5- to 6-pound pumpkin**
- **½ cup chopped onion (about 1 medium)**
- **½ cup thin slices celery (about 1 medium stalk)**
- **2 tablespoons reduced-calorie margarine**
- **1½ cups cooked brown rice**
- **½ cup cooked wild rice**
- **2 slices whole wheat bread, cut into cubes**
- **¼ cup currants or raisins**
- **1 teaspoon salt**
- **¼ teaspoon pepper**
- **1 cup unsweetened apple cider**

Heat oven to 375°. Cut 1 inch slice off top of pumpkin to form lid. Remove seeds and fibers from pumpkin. Cook onion and celery in margarine in 10-inch skillet until onion and celery are softened. Stir in remaining ingredients except cider. Fill pumpkin with rice mixture. Pour cider over filling. Cover with pumpkin lid.

Place pumpkin in ungreased square pan, 8 × 8 × 2 or 9 × 9 × 2 inches. Bake about 2 hours or until pumpkin is tender. Let stand about 15 minutes. To serve, remove lid. Cut pumpkin into wedges.

Vegetables and Hominy

———	Per Serving	———
Calories	180	Fat	1 g (9 calories)
Protein	9 g	Cholesterol	0 mg
Carbohydrate	36 g	Sodium	390 mg

4 Servings, about 1½ cups each

- **1 package (10 ounces) frozen lima beans**
- **½ cup water**
- **1 cup chopped onion (about 1 large)**
- **3 medium zucchini, cut lengthwise in half then crosswise into ¼ inch slices**
- **3 cups chopped tomatoes (about 3 large)**
- **1 can (14½ ounces) hominy, drained**
- **1 tablespoon chopped fresh or 1 teaspoon dried basil leaves**
- **1 tablespoon chili powder**
- **½ teaspoon salt**
- **⅛ teaspoon pepper**

Cook lima beans as directed on package—except use Dutch oven and add ½ cup additional water and the onion; drain. Stir in remaining ingredients. Cook uncovered over medium heat 5 to 10 minutes, stirring occasionally, until zucchini is crisp-tender.

MOROCCAN GARBANZO BEANS WITH RAISINS

Per Serving			
Calories	335	Fat	5 g (45 calories)
Protein	8 g	Cholesterol	0 mg
Carbohydrate	66 g	Sodium	400 mg

4 Servings, about 1¼ cups each

- **1 large onion, sliced**
- **½ cup chopped onion (about 1 medium)**
- **1 clove garlic, finely chopped**
- **2 tablespoons peanut oil**
- **1 cup diced acorn or butternut squash**
- **1 cup chicken broth**
- **¼ cup raisins**
- **1 teaspoon ground turmeric**
- **1 teaspoon ground cinnamon**
- **½ teaspoon ground ginger**
- **1 can (15 ounces) garbanzo beans, drained**
- **2 cups hot cooked rice**

Cook onions and garlic in oil in 3-quart saucepan about 7 minutes, stirring frequently, until tender. Stir in remaining ingredients except garbanzo beans and rice. Heat to boiling; reduce heat. Cover and simmer about 8 minutes, stirring occasionally, until squash is tender. Stir in garbanzo beans. Serve over rice.

CURRIED LENTILS AND BARLEY

Per Serving			
Calories	205	Fat	3 g (27 calories)
Protein	6 g	Cholesterol	0 mg
Carbohydrate	38 g	Sodium	470 mg

4 Servings, about 1 cup each

- **2 teaspoons vegetable oil**
- **½ cup chopped onion (about 1 medium)**
- **⅓ cup coarsely chopped red or green bell pepper**
- **3½ cups water**
- **½ cup uncooked barley**
- **1½ teaspoons curry powder**
- **¾ teaspoon salt**
- **1 cup thinly sliced carrots (about 2 large)**
- **¾ cup dried lentils, sorted and rinsed**
- **½ cup plain nonfat yogurt**
- **¼ cup chutney**

Heat oil in 3-quart saucepan over medium heat. Cook onion and bell pepper about 3 minutes, stirring occasionally, until softened. Stir in water, barley, curry powder and salt. Heat to boiling; reduce heat. Cover and simmer 15 minutes.

Stir in carrots and lentils. Heat to boiling; reduce heat. Cover and simmer 40 to 45 minutes, stirring occasionally, until lentils are tender and liquid is absorbed. Mix yogurt and chutney. Serve with lentils and barley.

CHAPTER 7
HEARTY SALADS

Fajita Salad (page 140)

Tuna-Couscous Salad

Per Serving			
Calories	320	Fat 11 g (99 calories)	
Protein	20 g	Cholesterol	45 mg
Carbohydrate	34 g	Sodium	670 mg

6 Servings, about 1 cup each

1 cup uncooked couscous

¼ cup sliced green onions with tops (about 2 medium)

2 cans (6½ ounces each) solid white tuna in water, drained

1 package (9 ounces) frozen cut green beans, thawed and drained

1 can (8 ounces) sliced water chestnuts, drained

½ cup reduced-calorie mayonnaise or salad dressing

½ cup plain nonfat yogurt

2 tablespoons cider vinegar

2 tablespoons chopped fresh or 2 teaspoons dried basil leaves

¼ teaspoon salt

3 cups bite-size pieces greens (spinach, leaf lettuce, romaine)

1 large tomato, cut into 12 wedges

Cook couscous as directed on package—except omit salt and margarine. Mix couscous, onions, tuna, green beans and water chestnuts in medium bowl. Mix remaining ingredients except greens and tomato wedges in separate bowl. Stir into couscous mixture. Cover and refrigerate about 3 hours or until chilled. Serve on greens; garnish with tomato wedges.

Tuna-Bean Salad

Try red, orange, yellow, or purple bell peppers for interesting color and flavor variations in this hearty salad.

Per Serving			
Calories	345	Fat 16 g (144 calories)	
Protein	23 g	Cholesterol	30 mg
Carbohydrate	29 g	Sodium	670 mg

6 Servings, about 1 cup each

Basil Dressing (page 125)

3 medium green bell peppers

2 cans (16 ounces each) cannellini or great northern beans, drained

2 cans (6½ ounces each) tuna in water, drained

⅓ cup sliced ripe olives

1 bunch leaf lettuce

1 medium tomato, cut into 16 wedges

Prepare Basil Dressing. Set oven control to broil. Place bell peppers on rack in broiler pan. Broil with tops 4 to 5 inches from heat about 5 minutes on each side or until skin blisters and browns. Wrap in towel; let stand 5 minutes. Remove skin, stems, seeds and membranes from peppers. Cut peppers into ¼-inch slices.

Toss peppers, beans, tuna, olives and Basil Dressing. Cover and refrigerate at least 4 hours, stirring occasionally. Spoon onto lettuce leaves; garnish with tomato wedges.

BASIL DRESSING

½ teaspoon grated lemon peel

⅓ cup lemon juice

¼ cup olive oil

2 tablespoons chopped fresh parsley

1 tablespoon chopped fresh or 1 teaspoon dried basil leaves

1 tablespoon Dijon mustard

½ teaspoon salt

Shake all ingredients in tightly covered container.

SALMON-SQUASH SALADS

Per Serving			
Calories	170	Fat 10 g (90 calories)	
Protein	14 g	Cholesterol	25 mg
Carbohydrate	7 g	Sodium	530 mg

6 Servings, about 1 cup each

Sesame Dressing (right)

1½ cups thinly sliced zucchini (about 1 small)

1½ cups thinly sliced yellow summer squash (about 1 small)

1 cup sliced celery (about 2 medium stalks)

1 small onion, sliced and separated into rings

1 cup sliced mushrooms (about 3 ounces)

Lettuce cups or leaves

1 can (15½ ounces) salmon, chilled, drained and flaked

12 cherry tomatoes

Prepare Sesame Dressing. Toss zucchini, summer squash, celery, onion and mushrooms. Place lettuce cups on each of 6 salad plates. Spoon vegetable mixture into lettuce cups. Place salmon on center of vegetable mixture. Top each with 2 cherry tomatoes. Spoon Sesame Dressing over salads.

SESAME DRESSING

1 tablespoon sesame seed

⅓ cup white wine vinegar

1 tablespoon sugar

2 tablespoons olive or vegetable oil

1 teaspoon dry mustard

½ teaspoon salt

1 large clove garlic, crushed

Cook sesame seed over medium heat, stirring frequently, until golden brown; cool. Shake seed and remaining ingredients in tightly covered container. Refrigerate about 2 hours or until chilled. Remove garlic and shake dressing before serving.

Tuna-Couscous Salad (page 124)

Salmon-Squash Salad (page 125)

SALMON AND GRAPEFRUIT SALAD

Pare grapefruit by cutting off the peel, including the white membrane. Section by using a knife to separate each section from the membrane.

Per Serving			
Calories	185	Fat	7 g (63 calories)
Protein	22 g	Cholesterol	40 mg
Carbohydrate	7 g	Sodium	1100 mg

4 Servings

- **1 container (8 ounces) plain nonfat yogurt**
- **1 tablespoon grated grapefruit peel**
- **½ teaspoon salt**
- **3 cups bite-size pieces greens (spinach, romaine, iceberg lettuce)**
- **1 tablespoon tarragon vinegar**
- **½ teaspoon seasoned salt**
- **1 cup thin diagonal slices celery (about 2 medium stalks)**
- **1 grapefruit, pared and sectioned**
- **1 can (16 ounces) salmon, drained and flaked**
- **Salad greens**

Mix yogurt, grapefruit peel and salt. Cover and refrigerate until serving time. Toss remaining ingredients. Serve with dressing on salad greens.

SEAFOOD TABBOULEH

Per Serving			
Calories	235	Fat	8 g (72 calories)
Protein	15 g	Cholesterol	85 mg
Carbohydrate	27 g	Sodium	230 mg

4 Servings, about 1¼ cups each

- **¾ cup uncooked bulgur**
- **¼ cup unsweetened apple juice**
- **3 tablespoons lemon juice**
- **2 tablespoons olive or vegetable oil**
- **¼ teaspoon salt**
- **⅛ teaspoon pepper**
- **2 cloves garlic, finely chopped**
- **1 cup chopped seeded unpared cucumber (about 1 small)**
- **½ cup chopped fresh parsley**
- **1 cup chopped tomato (about 1 large)**
- **½ cup sliced green onions with tops (about 4 medium)**
- **2 cans (4½ ounces each) medium shrimp, drained**

Rinse and drain bulgur. Shake apple juice, lemon juice, oil, salt, pepper and garlic in tightly covered container. Mix bulgur and remaining ingredients in medium bowl. Pour apple juice mixture over bulgur mixture; toss. Cover and refrigerate about 3 hours or until chilled. Stir before serving. Sprinkle with freshly ground pepper if desired.

If YOU LIKE MAYONNAISE AND SALAD DRESSING, but are confused by the choices available, here's an easy lesson:

▲ Regular mayonnaise or salad dressing contains 60 to 100 calories per tablespoon.

▲ Reduced-calorie, light or "lite" mayonnaise contains 20 to 50 calories per tablespoon.

▲ Regular, cholesterol-free mayonnaise and salad dressing has 60 to 100 calories per tablespoon but does not contain cholesterol because the egg yolk has been omitted.

▲ Reduced-calorie, light or "lite" cholesterol-free mayonnaise contains 20 to 50 calories per tablespoon and also has no cholesterol.

▲ Vinaigrette-type bottled salad dressings are made from vegetable oils and are cholesterol-free but can contain 45 to 100 calories and 4 to 9 grams of fat per tablespoon. The total oil content has been cut in the reduced-calorie counterparts, which in many cases are oil-free. Recipes for salad dressings typically use 3 parts oil to 1 part vinegar. Try using 1 part oil to 1 part vinegar. Mild vinegars with flavorings such as balsamic or raspberry reduce tartness.

▲ Creamy bottled salad dressings vary widely in fat content, cholesterol and calorie counts. Many bottled dressings average 60 to 80 calories and 6 to 8 grams of fat per tablespoon, while the reduced-calorie versions are one-quarter to one-half that amount.

CREAMY FISH AND FRUIT SALAD

This spicy jalapeño dressing complements the fruit beautifully. Great with breadsticks!

Per Serving			
Calories	340	Fat 12 g (108 calories)	
Protein	24 g	Cholesterol	70 mg
Carbohydrate	37 g	Sodium	190 mg

4 Servings

- 1 pound orange roughy or other lean fish fillets
- 3 cups bite-size pieces salad greens (spinach, romaine, iceberg lettuce)
- 1 medium cantaloupe or Persian melon (about 1½ pounds), pared and cut into thin wedges
- 2 cups bite-size pieces pineapple (about ½ medium)
- ½ pound seedless grapes, divided into small bunches
- Creamy Jalapeño Dressing (right)
- 2 tablespoons sliced green onions with tops (about 1 medium)

Set oven control to broil. Place fish fillets on rack in broiler pan. Broil with tops about 4 inches from heat 5 to 6 minutes or until fish flakes easily with fork (do not turn); cool. Flake fish. Place salad greens on serving platter or 4 salad plates. Arrange cantaloupe, pineapple, grapes and fish on greens. Top with Creamy Jalapeño Dressing. Sprinkle with onions.

CREAMY JALAPEÑO DRESSING

- ¼ cup reduced-calorie mayonnaise or salad dressing
- ¼ cup plain nonfat yogurt or low-fat sour cream
- ½ jalapeño chili, seeded and coarsely chopped

Place all ingredients in blender or food processor. Cover and blend or process until smooth.

SALADE NIÇOISE

Per Serving			
Calories	255	Fat 15 g (135 calories)	
Protein	20 g	Cholesterol	130 mg
Carbohydrate	12 g	Sodium	880 mg

4 Servings

- 1 package (9 ounces) frozen French-style or Italian-style green beans*
- Herb Vinaigrette Dressing (page 131)
- 1 head Boston lettuce, torn into bite-size pieces
- 2 tomatoes, cut into sixths
- 2 hard-cooked eggs, cut into fourths
- 1 can (6½ ounces) tuna in water, drained
- 8 pitted ripe olives
- 1 can (about 2 ounces) anchovy fillets
- Chopped fresh parsley

Cook beans as directed on package; drain. Cover and refrigerate at least 1 hour. Prepare Herb Vinaigrette Dressing.

Place lettuce in salad bowl; arrange beans, tomatoes and eggs around edge. Mound tuna in center. Garnish with olives, anchovies and parsley.

HERB VINAIGRETTE DRESSING

⅓ cup unsweetened apple juice

¼ cup vinegar

2 tablespoons olive or vegetable oil

1 tablespoon finely chopped green onion

1 tablespoon chopped fresh parsley

1 tablespoon chopped fresh herb (tarragon, rosemary, basil, oregano, thyme or marjoram)

Shake all ingredients in tightly covered container; refrigerate.

*¾ pound fresh green beans, cooked (about 2 cups), can be substituted for the frozen green beans.

ANTIPASTO TERRINE

	Per Serving		
Calories	270	Fat 14 g (126 calories)	
Protein	19 g	Cholesterol	85 mg
Carbohydrate	15 g	Sodium	1200 mg

6 Servings

2 envelopes unflavored gelatin

½ cup cold water

2⅔ cups chicken broth

2 hard-cooked eggs, thinly sliced

3½ ounces coarsely chopped pepperoni

1½ cups cooked tiny pasta rings (anellini)

½ cup sliced ripe olives

1 cup finely chopped zucchini (about 1 medium)

1 jar (4 ounces) diced pimientos, drained

1 can (6½ ounces) tuna in water, drained

2 teaspoons chopped fresh or 1 teaspoon dried oregano leaves

2 teaspoons chopped fresh or 1 teaspoon dried basil leaves

½ cup oil-free Italian dressing

Sprinkle gelatin on cold water in 2-quart saucepan to soften. Heat over low heat, stirring constantly, until gelatin is dissolved; remove from heat. Stir in chicken broth. Pour ⅓ cup mixture into loaf pan, $9 \times 5 \times 3$ inches; reserve remaining gelatin mixture. Refrigerate mixture in pan about 10 minutes or until almost set. Arrange 5 egg slices and the pepperoni over top. Chop remaining egg slices; reserve.

Layer in order pasta, olives, zucchini, reserved chopped egg, pimientos and tuna over pepperoni, sprinkling layers with oregano and basil. Stir dressing into reserved gelatin mixture. Pour carefully over tuna. Cover and refrigerate about 4 hours or until firm. Garnish with salad greens if desired.

DILLED SHRIMP IN MELON SALAD

Cut a thin slice off the bottom of each melon half and it will be stable.

─────── Per Serving ───────			
Calories	205	Fat	7 g (63 calories)
Protein	15 g	Cholesterol	215 mg
Carbohydrate	21 g	Sodium	200 mg

4 Servings

- **2 small honeydew melons or canta-loupe, chilled**
- **1 cup thinly sliced pared or unpared cucumber (about 1 small)**
- **¾ pound frozen cooked medium shrimp, thawed and drained**
- **⅓ cup plain nonfat yogurt**
- **2 tablespoons reduced-calorie mayonnaise or salad dressing**
- **2 teaspoons chopped fresh or ½ teaspoon dried dill weed**
- **1 teaspoon sugar**
- **½ teaspoon grated lemon peel**
- **2 tablespoons sliced almonds**

Cut each melon in half, using a deep zigzag cut.* Remove seeds. Scoop melon from each half, leaving a 1-inch rim around the top. Chop melon and drain thoroughly.

Mix melon, cucumber and shrimp. Mix remaining ingredients except almonds; toss with melon mixture. Spoon one-fourth of the filling into each shell. Sprinkle with almonds. Serve immediately.

*To cut melon, use toothpick to mark the top and bottom point of each zigzag just above and below the center of the melon, keeping marks 1 inch apart. Insert paring knife diagonally between an adjacent top and bottom mark, pushing the knife into the center of the melon. Repeat cutting between all marks. Pull the halves apart.

CURRIED CHICKEN AND RICE SALAD

You can vary this salad so many ways by using different varieties—and colors—of grapes, apples and raisins.

─────── Per Serving ───────			
Calories	320	Fat	4 g (36 calories)
Protein	19 g	Cholesterol	45 mg
Carbohydrate	51 g	Sodium	160 mg

4 Servings, about 1½ cups each

- **2 cups cooked rice**
- **1½ cups cut-up cooked chicken or pork (about 8 ounces)**
- **1 cup seedless green or red grapes, cut into halves**
- **1 cup chopped unpared tart eating apple (about 1 medium)**
- **1 cup frozen green peas, thawed**
- **2 tablespoons raisins**
- **¾ cup plain nonfat yogurt**
- **2 tablespoons chutney**
- **1½ teaspoons curry powder**

Mix rice, chicken, grapes, apple, peas and raisins in large bowl. Mix remaining ingredients; toss with rice mixture. Cover and refrigerate about 3 hours or until chilled.

WILTED SPINACH AND CHICKEN SALAD

──────── Per Serving ────────			
Calories	295	Fat 22 g (198 calories)	
Protein	16 g	Cholesterol	60 mg
Carbohydrate	10 g	Sodium	460 mg

4 Servings, about 3 cups each

1 skinless boneless whole chicken breast (about ½ pound)

4 slices bacon

1 tablespoon sesame seed

¼ cup vinegar

2 teaspoons sugar

1 teaspoon cornstarch

½ teaspoon salt

¼ teaspoon pepper

1 pound spinach

½ small red onion, thinly sliced

Cut chicken breast into 1-inch pieces; reserve. Cook bacon in Dutch oven over medium heat until crisp. Drain bacon, reserving fat in Dutch oven. Crumble bacon. Stir chicken and sesame seed into fat in Dutch oven. Cook over medium heat 6 to 7 minutes, stirring occasionally, until chicken is white.

Mix vinegar, sugar, cornstarch, salt and pepper. Stir into chicken mixture. Heat to boiling, stirring constantly. Boil and stir 1 minute; remove from heat. Add spinach and onion. Toss 2 to 3 minutes or until spinach is wilted. Sprinkle with bacon. Serve immediately.

MEXICAN CHICKEN SALAD

Capers add zest to this chicken salad, but they are pickled in a salty brine. If you'd like to cut down on salt, rinse the capers before adding to salad.

──────── Per Serving ────────			
Calories	305	Fat 20 g (180 calories)	
Protein	21 g	Cholesterol	75 mg
Carbohydrate	11 g	Sodium	190 mg

4 Servings, about 1 cup each

2 cups cut-up cooked chicken (about 10 ounces)

¼ cup low-fat sour cream

¼ cup reduced-calorie mayonnaise or salad dressing

¼ cup finely chopped carrot

2 tablespoons chopped fresh cilantro

2 tablespoons capers

2 tablespoons chopped pimiento

2 tablespoons lime juice

½ teaspoon ground cumin

2 teaspoons chopped fresh or ½ teaspoon dried oregano leaves

¼ cup chopped onion (about 1 small)

Lettuce leaves

1 avocado, peeled and cut into wedges

Paprika

Toss all ingredients except lettuce, avocado and paprika. Serve on lettuce with avocado; sprinkle with paprika.

HOT CHICKEN SALAD WITH PLUM SAUCE

Per Serving			
Calories	220	Fat	4 g (36 calories)
Protein	28 g	Cholesterol	65 mg
Carbohydrate	16 g	Sodium	140 mg

4 Servings

- **2 teaspoons olive or vegetable oil**
- **4 skinless boneless chicken breast halves (about 1 pound)**
- **1 can (16 ounces) purple plums in juice, rinsed, drained and pitted**
- **1 tablespoon lemon juice**
- **2 teaspoons packed brown sugar**
- **¼ teaspoon ground ginger**
- **⅛ teaspoon crushed red pepper**
- **1 clove garlic**
- **4 cups shredded Chinese cabbage**
- **1 cup bean sprouts (about 2 ounces)**
- **1 tablespoon thinly sliced green onion with top (about ½ medium)**

Heat oil in 10-inch nonstick skillet over medium heat. Cook chicken breast halves, turning once, about 10 minutes or until done.

Place remaining ingredients except cabbage, bean sprouts and onion in blender or food processor. Cover and blend on high speed or process about 30 seconds or until smooth. Heat sauce if desired.

Arrange cabbage, bean sprouts and onion on 4 serving plates. Top with chicken. Spoon plum sauce over chicken.

CHICKEN AND TORTELLINI SALAD

Per Serving			
Calories	270	Fat	8 g (72 calories)
Protein	15 g	Cholesterol	30 mg
Carbohydrate	31 g	Sodium	220 mg

4 Servings, about 2¾ cups each

- **1 package (8 ounces) cheese-filled tortellini**
- **1½ cups cut-up cooked chicken or turkey (about 8 ounces)**
- **1 tablespoon chopped fresh or 1 teaspoon dried tarragon leaves**
- **⅓ cup dry white wine or chicken broth**
- **2 tablespoons olive or vegetable oil**
- **2 tablespoons lemon juice**
- **1 teaspoon sugar**
- **½ teaspoon salt**
- **¼ teaspoon pepper**
- **3 cups bite-size pieces greens (spinach, leaf lettuce, romaine)**
- **1 small red or green bell pepper, cut into ½-inch squares**

Cook tortellini as directed on package; drain. Rinse with cold water; drain. Mix tortellini and chicken in large bowl.

Shake tarragon, wine, oil, lemon juice, sugar, salt and pepper in tightly covered container. Stir into tortellini mixture. Cover and refrigerate at least 2 hours. Toss tortellini mixture with greens and bell pepper just before serving.

Hot Chicken Salad with Plum Sauce

Chicken and Fruit Salad with Green Chili Dressing

Per Serving			
Calories	345	Fat 19 g (171 calories)	
Protein	20 g	Cholesterol	80 mg
Carbohydrate	25 g	Sodium	400 mg

4 Servings, about 2 cups each

3 cups bite-size pieces greens (spinach, romaine, iceberg lettuce) and shredded red cabbage

2 cups cubed cooked chicken or turkey (about 10 ounces)

2 cups bite-size pieces honeydew, cantaloupe, casaba or Spanish melon (about 1½ pounds unpared melon)

2 cups bite-size pieces pineapple (about ½ medium)

1 cup julienne strips jicama (about ½ small) or thinly sliced celery (about 2 medium stalks)

Green Chili Dressing (right)

Arrange salad greens and cabbage on platter or 4 salad plates. Top with chicken, melon, pineapple and jicama. Garnish with lime slices and cilantro sprigs if desired. Serve with Green Chili Dressing.

Green Chili Dressing

1 cup reduced-calorie mayonnaise or salad dressing

1 to 2 tablespoons finely chopped mild or hot green chilies

2 tablespoons lime juice

1 green onion with top, thinly sliced, or 2 tablespoons snipped fresh cilantro

Mix all ingredients.

Chicken and Fruit Salad with Green Chili Dressing

If YOU LOVE SOUR CREAM, as well as mayonnaise, salad dressing or flavored yogurt, try the following tips to reduce calories.

▲ You can purchase a wide selection of high-quality reduced-calorie, low-fat and nonfat products at your supermarket. Calories can be reduced even further if the reduced-calorie versions of these foods are mixed with equal parts of nonfat plain yogurt. You'll cut calories without losing taste!

▲ To control calories in flavored yogurts, mix your own. Purchase nonfat plain yogurt and flavor it yourself by adding artificial sweetener, vanilla, cut-up or mashed fresh fruit, sugar-free fruit preserves, fruit juice concentrate, instant fruit drink mix or instant coffee. Eat yogurt plain, with a muffin, over cereal, as a main dish as salad dressing, with fresh fruit or on top of angel food cake. It's versatile, healthful and will satisfy the desire for something creamy and filling.

TURKEY-FRUIT SALAD

To serve, you can leave the turkey in slices, or cut it up into peices, whichever you prefer.

———	Per Serving	———	
Calories	290	Fat 13 g (117 calories)	
Protein	27 g	Cholesterol	80 mg
Carbohydrate	17 g	Sodium	95 mg

4 Servings

2 teaspoons olive or vegetable oil

1 tablespoon chopped fresh or 1 teaspoon dried mint leaves

Freshly ground pepper

1 pound skinless boneless turkey breast slices

¼ cup low-fat sour cream

¼ cup plain nonfat yogurt

1 teaspoon grated orange peel

1 tablespoon orange juice

1 teaspoon chopped fresh or ¼ teaspoon dried mint leaves

1 teaspoon sugar

½ small cantaloupe or honeydew melon, sliced

1 cup sliced strawberries

1 kiwifruit, pared and sliced

Heat oil in 10-inch nonstick skillet over medium-high heat. Sprinkle 1 tablespoon mint and the pepper evenly over turkey breast slices. Sauté turkey 3 to 4 minutes, turning once, until no longer pink. Cover and refrigerate about 1 hour or until chilled.

Mix remaining ingredients except fruit; cover and refrigerate.

Arrange turkey slices and fruit on 4 serving plates. Top with sour cream mixture. Garnish with mint leaves if desired.

TURKEY TACO SALAD

Per Serving			
Calories	310	Fat 14 g (126 calories)	
Protein	21 g	Cholesterol	60 mg
Carbohydrate	24 g	Sodium	780 mg

4 Servings, about 1¾ cups each

3 flour tortillas (about 8 inches in diameter)

½ pound ground turkey

⅓ cup water

1 to 2 teaspoons chili powder

½ teaspoon salt

¼ teaspoon garlic powder

¼ teaspoon ground red pepper (cayenne)

1 can (8 ounces) kidney beans, drained

5 cups shredded lettuce

1 cup chopped tomato (about 1 large)

½ cup shredded low-fat Monterey Jack cheese (2 ounces)

¼ cup chopped onion (about 1 small)

¼ cup reduced-calorie Thousand Island dressing

¼ cup low-fat sour cream

4 pitted ripe olives, sliced

Heat oven to 400°. Cut each tortilla into 12 wedges or about 3 × ¼-inch strips. Place in ungreased jelly roll pan, 15½ × 10½ × 1 inch. Bake 6 to 8 minutes, stirring at least once, until golden brown and crisp; cool.

Cook ground turkey in 10-inch nonstick skillet, stirring occasionally, until no longer pink. Stir in water, chili powder, salt, garlic powder, red pepper and kidney beans. Heat to boiling; reduce heat. Simmer uncovered 2 to 3 minutes, stirring occasionally, until liquid is absorbed. Cool 10 minutes.

Mix lettuce, tomato, cheese and onion in large bowl; toss with Thousand Island dressing. Divide among 4 salad plates. Top each salad with about ½ cup turkey mixture. Arrange tortilla wedges around salad. Garnish with sour cream and olives.

Fajita Salad

Here's a low-calorie version of a favorite Tex-Mex dish.

Per Serving			
Calories	315	Fat 16 g (144 calories)	
Protein	21 g	Cholesterol	55 mg
Carbohydrate	22 g	Sodium	320 mg

4 Servings

Corn Chips (right)

¾-pound lean beef boneless sirloin steak

2 teaspoons vegetable oil

2 medium bell peppers, cut into strips

1 small onion, thinly sliced

1 tablespoon vegetable oil

3 tablespoons red wine vinegar

1 tablespoon lime juice

1 teaspoon chopped fresh or ½ teaspoon dried oregano leaves

¾ teaspoon chili powder

¼ teaspoon salt

1 clove garlic, finely chopped

4 cups bite-size pieces greens (spinach, romaine, iceberg lettuce)

¼ cup nonfat plain yogurt

Prepare Corn Chips. Trim fat from beef steak. Cut beef with grain into 2-inch strips. Cut strips across grain into ⅛-inch slices. Heat 2 teaspoons oil in 10-inch nonstick skillet over medium-high heat. Sauté beef about 3 minutes, or until no longer pink. Remove beef from skillet. Add bell peppers and onion to skillet. Sauté about 3 minutes, or until crisp-tender. Mix beef and vegetables.

Shake remaining ingredients except greens and yogurt in tightly covered container. Place greens on serving plate. Top with beef mixture. Pour dressing over salad. Top with yogurt. Serve with Corn Chips.

Corn Chips

4 corn tortillas (about 6 inches in diameter)

1 tablespoon reduced-calorie margarine, melted

⅛ teaspoon salt

Heat oven to 400°. Brush tortillas with margarine; sprinkle with salt. Cut each tortilla into 10 pieces. Arrange in ungreased jelly roll pan, 15½ × 10½ × 1 inch. Bake 5 to 6 minutes or until crisp. (Chips will crisp as they cool.)

BEEF AND EGGPLANT SALAD

——— Per Serving ———			
Calories	190	Fat 10 g (90 calories)	
Protein	19 g	Cholesterol	55 mg
Carbohydrate	7 g	Sodium	330 mg

8 Servings, about ¾ cup each

1 cup water

½ teaspoon salt

1 medium eggplant (about 1½ pounds), cut into ¾-inch cubes

3 tablespoons olive or vegetable oil

2 tablespoons lemon juice

1 tablespoon chopped fresh or 1 teaspoon dried oregano leaves

½ teaspoon salt

¼ teaspoon pepper

1 pound cold roast beef, cut into julienne strips

1 tablespoon chopped fresh parsley

1 medium tomato, cut into 8 wedges

8 Greek or large pitted ripe olives

Heat water and ½ teaspoon salt to boiling in 3-quart saucepan. Add eggplant cubes. Cover and heat to boiling; reduce heat. Simmer about 10 minutes or until tender; drain.

Place eggplant in glass or plastic bowl. Mix oil, lemon juice, oregano, ½ teaspoon salt and the pepper. Pour over eggplant; toss. Cover and refrigerate at least 5 hours.

Arrange beef strips on platter or 8 serving plates on lettuce leaves if desired. Top with eggplant. Sprinkle eggplant with parsley. Garnish with tomato wedges and olives.

HAM WALDORF SALAD

——— Per Serving ———			
Calories	220	Fat 9 g (81 calories)	
Protein	16 g	Cholesterol	20 mg
Carbohydrate	21 g	Sodium	700 mg

6 Servings, about 1 cup each

¾ cup plain nonfat yogurt

½ teaspoon ground nutmeg

½ teaspoon Worcestershire sauce

2½ cups cut-up fully cooked smoked extra-lean ham (about 12 ounces)

2 cups coarsely chopped unpared eating apples (about 2 medium)

1 cup sliced celery (about 2 medium stalks)

1 cup seedles red or green grapes

½ cup coarsely chopped walnuts

¼ cup sliced green onions with tops

Lettuce

1 medium pared or unpared eating apple, cut into wedges

Mix yogurt, nutmeg and Worcestershire sauce. Toss with remaining ingredients except lettuce and apple wedges. Cover and refrigerate at least 2 hours. Serve on lettuce; garnish with apple wedges.

PORK AND MANGO SALAD

If you like, use skinless chicken instead of pork, and you'll save about 45 calories per serving.

Per Serving			
Calories	290	Fat 13 g (117 calories)	
Protein	19 g	Cholesterol	50 mg
Carbohydrate	27 g	Sodium	70 mg

4 Servings

1 large mango or papaya

½ cup plain nonfat yogurt

1 teaspoon sugar

¼ teaspoon ground ginger

4 cups shredded Boston or iceberg lettuce

2 cups julienne strips cooked lean pork (about 8 ounces)

1 cup orange sections (about 2 medium)

½ avocado, peeled and thinly sliced

Cut mango in half and peel. Mash enough mango to measure ¼ cup; cut remaining mango into thin slices. Mix mashed mango, yogurt, sugar and ginger.

Place 1 cup lettuce on each of 4 salad plates. Arrange mango slices, pork, oranges and avocado on lettuce. Top each salad with mango mixture.

TEX-MEX EGG SALAD

This very special egg salad turns the ho-hum into the highly delicious!

Per Serving			
Calories	205	Fat 14 g (126 calories)	
Protein	10 g	Cholesterol	235 mg
Carbohydrate	9 g	Sodium	380 mg

4 Servings

4 hard-cooked eggs, chopped

¼ cup reduced-calorie mayonnaise or salad dressing

¼ cup low-fat sour cream

¼ cup diced Monterey Jack cheese (1 ounce)

2 tablespoons chopped green onion with top (about 1 medium)

2 teaspoons chopped fresh cilantro or parsley

¼ teaspoon salt

1 jalapeño chili, seeded and finely chopped

4 medium tomatoes

Mix all ingredients except tomatoes. Cut stem ends from tomatoes. Place tomatoes cut sides down. Cut into sixths to within ½ inch of bottom. Carefully spread out sections. Spoon about ½ cup salad into each tomato.

COUNTING CALORIES

BEVERAGES

	CALORIES
Alcoholic	
Beer (12 ounces)	145
Gin (1 ounce)	75
Mixed drinks (about 1½ ounces)	155
Wine (4 ounces)	85
Carbonated (8 ounces)	
Cola	105
Ginger ale	80
Lemonade	105
Sugar-free	0
Tonic water	80
Coffee (8 ounces)	
Black	5
With 2 teaspoons each cream and sugar	55
Milk type (8 ounces)	
Cocoa with milk	220
Malted milk shake, chocolate	285
Milk	
Buttermilk, skim	85
Evaporated	340
Evaporated skim	200
Low-fat, 2%	120
Skim	85
Whole	150
Tea (8 ounces)	2

BREADS, CEREAL AND GRAIN PRODUCTS

	CALORIES
Bagel, 1 (plain)	120
Biscuit (2-inch)	155
Breads (1-ounce slice raisin, white or whole wheat)	65
Cereals	
Cooked (½ cup) Oatmeal	75
Dry (1 cup)	
Flaked cereal, bran, corn and wheat	110
Puffed cereal, rice and wheat	50
Wheat, shredded (1 biscuit)	85
Cornbread (2-inch square)	110
Crackers	
Graham (2½-inch square)	25
Saltine (2-inch square)	15

	CALORIES
Croissant (1 small plain)	110
Dried Beans and Lentils (½ cup cooked)	105
English Muffin (1 plain)	70
Flour, all-purpose (1 tablespoon)	25
Muffin (2½-inch)	175
Pancake (4-inch)	70
Pasta (½ cup cooked)	100
Rice (½ cup cooked), regular long grain	130
Rice, wild (½ cup cooked)	85
Rice cake (4-inch)	30
Rolls (1 average)	
Danish	350
Frankfurter or hamburger	120
Hard	155
Tortilla (8-inch)	95
Waffle (3½-inch square), frozen	95
Wheat germ (¼ cup)	110
Zwieback (1 piece)	30

CHEESE

	CALORIES
American (1 ounce)	105
Cheddar (1 ounce)	115
Cottage (¼ cup)	55
Cream (1 ounce)	100
Mozzarella, part-skin (1 ounce)	70
Neufchâtel (1 ounce)	75
Parmesan (1 ounce)	110
Parmesan (1 tablespoon grated)	25
Spread (1 ounce)	80
Swiss (1 ounce)	105

DESSERTS

	CALORIES
Apple Betty (½ cup)	160
Brownies (2-inch square)	150
Cake	
Angel Food (1/12, plain 10-inch)	125
Chocolate/Chocolate icing (1/12, 2-layer)	235
Cupcake, plain (2½-inch)	50
Pound (½-inch slice)	140
Cheesecake, New York–style (1/20)	430
Cookies	

DESSERTS *(cont.)*	CALORIES
Chocolate Chip (1¾-inch)	90
Gingersnap (2-inch)	55
Oatmeal with raisins (2½-inch)	90
Sandwich (1½-inch)	50
Shortbread (1½-inch square)	35
Sugar (3-inch)	55
Vanilla Wafer (1½-inch)	20
Custard (½ cup)	150
Doughnuts	
Plain cake or raised	165
Raised, jelly center	175
Eclair, custard filling chocolate icing	265
Gelatin (½ cup)	
Regular, fruit-flavored	80
Sugar-free, fruit-flavored	10
Gingerbread (2-inch square)	275
Ice Cream (½ cup)	
Premium (16% fat)	175
Regular (10% fat)	135
Ice Milk (½ cup)	
Hardened	90
Soft-serve	110
Pies (⅛, 9-inch)	
Custard	320
Fruit, 2-crust	425
Lemon Meringue	440
Pecan	560
Pumpkin	360
Pudding (½ cup)	
Bread with raisins	225
Chocolate, regular with whole milk	160
Chocolate, sugar-free with skim milk	65
Rice with raisins	245
Tapioca	150
Sherbet (½ cup)	135
Shortcake, strawberry	360

EGGS	CALORIES
Cooked, Hard or Soft	75
Fried or Scrambled	
(with 1 teaspoon margarine or butter)	90

FATS AND OILS (1 tablespoon)	CALORIES
Butter	100
Cream	
Half-and-half	202
Sour	25
Sour Half-and-half	20
Whipping	50
Lard	115
Margarine	
Reduced-calorie	60
Regular	100
Oil, vegetable	120
Salad dressings	
Blue Cheese	
reduced-calorie	15
regular	75
French	
reduced-calorie	20
regular	65
Mayonnaise	
reduced-calorie	40
regular	55
Thousand Island	
reduced-calorie	25
regular	60

FRUITS AND FRUIT JUICES

	CALORIES
Apple (2½-inch)	70
Apple Juice (½ cup)	60
Applesauce (½ cup)	
Canned, sweetened	95
Canned, unsweetened	55
Apricots	
Canned, in juice (½ cup)	35
Canned, in syrup (½ cup)	105
Fresh (3 medium)	50
Avocado (3½-inch × 4-inch, ½)	165
Banana (6 inches)	105
Blackberries, fresh (½ cup)	40
Blueberries, fresh (½ cup)	40

FRUITS AND FRUIT JUICES (cont.)	CALORIES		MEATS [Lean, well-trimmed (3 ounces cooked)]	CALORIES
Cantaloupe (5-inch, ½)	95		Beef	
Cherries			Chuck	200
Canned, in juice (½ cup)	45		Corned	215
Canned, in syrup (½ cup)	115		Ground beef	
Fresh sweet (½ cup)	50		grilled, lean	225
Coconut, shredded (½ cup)	175		grilled, regular	265
Cranberry sauce, sweetened (½ cup)	210		Liver, fried	185
Dates (3 medium)	70		Roast	
Fig, dried (1 large)	50		rib	195
Fruit Cocktail, sweetened (½ cup)	75		rump	180
Grapefruit (½ medium)	40		Steak	
Grapefruit Juice, canned (½ cup)	50		flank	210
Grape Juice, canned (½ cup)	80		porterhouse	185
Grapes, green seedless (½ cup)	30		round	190
Honeydew Melon (5-inch, ¼)	115		sirloin	180
Lemon Juice (1 tablespoon)	5		T-bone	180
Nectarine (2-inch)	65		Lamb	
Orange (2⅝-inch)	65		Chop, loin	180
Orange Juice, unsweetened (½ cup)	50		Roast	
Peach			leg	160
Canned, in juice (½ cup)	30		shoulder	175
Canned, in syrup (½ cup)	70		Pork	
Fresh (2-inch)	35		Chop, loin	220
Pear			Ham	
Canned, in juice (½ cup)	35		cured	145
Canned, in syrup (½ cup)	70		fresh	185
Fresh (3 × 2½-inch)	100		Roast, loin	195
Pineapple			Tenderloin	140
Canned, in juice (½ cup)	70		Veal	
Canned, in syrup (½ cup)	95		Chop, loin	200
Fresh (½ cup)	40		Cutlet	185
Juice, unsweetened (½ cup)	70		Roast	185
Plum, fresh (2-inch)	35		Miscellaneous	
Prune Juice (½ cup)	90		Bacon (2 medium slices), cooked crisp	70
Prunes (4 medium)	80		Bologna (1 ounce)	60
Pumpkin, canned (½ cup)	40		Braunschweiger (2 × ¼-inch slice)	65
Raisins, dry (2 tablespoons)	55		Frankfurter (2 ounces)	185
Raspberries, fresh (½ cup)	30		Pork link (2½ ounces)	265
Rhubarb, stewed, sweetened (½ cup)	140			
Strawberries (½ cup)			NUTS (¼ cup)	CALORIES
Fresh	25		Almonds	215
Frozen, sweetened	125		Brazil	230
Tangerine (2½-inch)	35		Cashews	195
Watermelon (1 cup diced pieces)	50		Hazelnuts	180

NUTS (¼ cup) *(cont.)*

	CALORIES
Peanuts	215
Pecans	180
Walnuts	195

POULTRY (3 ounces cooked)

	CALORIES
Chicken	
Breast, fried, with bone, no skin	160
Breast, roasted, no skin	140
Drumstick, fried, with bone, no skin	80
Drumstick, fried, with skin	120
Roasted, no skin	140
Goose, roasted, no skin	205
Turkey, roasted, no skin	145

SAUCES (2 tablespoons)

	CALORIES
Butterscotch	150
Cheese	40
Chili	30
Chocolate Fudge	65
Hollandaise	70
Lemon	35
Tartar	155
Tomato	10
White	50

SEAFOOD (3 ounces)

	CALORIES
Clams, canned	85
Cod, broiled	90
Crabmeat, canned	85
Fish Stick, batter-dipped	230
Halibut, broiled	120
Lobster, cooked	85
Oysters, raw (6 medium)	60
Salmon, pink, canned	120
Sardines, canned in oil	175
Scallops, cooked	115
Shrimp	
Canned	100
French-fried	205
Fresh, cooked	85

SEAFOOD (3 ounces) *(cont.)*

	CALORIES
Squid, French-fried	150
Tuna	
Canned in oil	160
Water-pack	115

SOUPS (made with water, 1 cup)

	CALORIES
Bean with Bacon	175
Beef Noodle	85
Bouillon	20
Clam Chowder	95
Cream of Chicken	115
Cream of Mushroom	130
Oyster Stew	60
Split Pea & Ham	190
Tomato	85
Vegetable-Beef	80

SWEETS

	CALORIES
Candies	
Carmels (1 medium)	40
Chocolate	
bar, plain (1 ounce)	155
kisses (7)	175
Fudge (1 ounce)	110
Gum Drops (8 small)	55
Jelly Beans (10)	65
Lollypop (2¼-inch)	110
Marshmallow (1 large)	25
Peanut Brittle (1 ounce)	125
Jams and Preserves (1 tablespoon)	55
Jellies (1 tablespoon)	55
Sugars (½ cup)	
Brown	415
Granulated	370
Powdered	245
Syrups (1 tablespoon)	
Chocolate-flavored	50
Corn	60
Honey	65
Maple	55
Molasses	45

VEGETABLES	CALORIES
Asparagus, cooked (½ cup)	20
Bamboo Shoots (½ cup)	20
Beans (½ cup)	
Baked, no pork	120
Green, cooked	20
Kidney, cooked	115
Lima, cooked	95
Beet Greens, cooked (½ cup)	15
Beets, cooked (½ cup)	25
Bell Pepper, raw (1 medium)	20
Broccoli, cooked (½ cup)	20
Brussels Sprouts, cooked (½ cup)	30
Cabbage (½ cup)	
Cooked	15
Raw	10
Carrots, raw or cooked (½ cup or one, 5½ × 1-inch)	25
Cauliflower, cooked (½ cup)	15
Celery (8 × ½-inch stalk)	5
Corn	
Canned, whole kernel (½ cup)	85
Cob (5 × 1¾-inch ear)	60
Cucumber (½ cup slices)	5
Eggplant, cooked (½ cup)	25
Kale, cooked (½ cup)	20
Lettuce, iceberg (5-inch, ¼)	20
Mushrooms, canned (¼ cup)	10
Fresh (½ cup)	10
Okra, cooked, 3 × ⅝ inches, 8 pods)	25
Onions	
Cooked (½ cup)	45
Green (6 small)	10
Parsnips, cooked (½ cup)	65
Peas, cooked (½ cup)	65
Potato	
Baked (2¼-inch)	100
French-fried (10 pieces, 2 × ½ inch)	155
Sweet (½ cup)	105
Radishes (4 small)	5
Rutabagas, cooked (½ cup)	30
Sauerkraut (½ cup)	20

VEGETABLES (cont.)	CALORIES
Spinach, cooked (½ cup)	20
Squash, cooked (½ cup)	
Summer	20
Winter	40
Tomato	
Canned (½ cup)	25
Fresh (3-inch)	25
Tomato Juice (½ cup)	20
Turnips, cooked (½ cup)	15
Water Chestnuts (4)	15

UNCLASSIFIED	CALORIES
Cocoa (1 tablespoon)	20
Chocolate, bitter (1 ounce)	140
Gelatin, unflavored (1 envelope)	25
Gelatin Pop, frozen	30
Gravy (1 tablespoon)	40
Herring, pickled (1 ounce)	60
Ice Cream Bar, chocolate-covered	150
Ketchup (1 tablespoon)	15
Mustard, prepared (1 teaspoon)	5
Olives	
Green (4 medium)	15
Ripe (4 small)	15
Peanut Butter (1 tablespoon)	95
Pickles	
Dill (1 whole)	10
Sweet (1 large)	50
Pizza, cheese (⅛, 14-inch)	155
Popcorn (1 cup)	
Added Oil	65
Hot-air Popped	45
Popsicle	70
Potato Chips (1 ounce)	150
Pretzels (1 ounce)	110
Vinegar (2 tablespoons)	5
Yogurt (1 cup)	
Fruit-flavored	245
Nonfat Plain	120
Plain	175

Metric Conversion Tables

DRY AND LIQUID MEASUREMENTS

Imperial	Metric
¼ teaspoon	1 mL
½ teaspoon	2 mL
1 teaspoon	5 mL
1 tablespoon	15 mL
2 tablespoons	25 mL
3 tablespoons	50 mL
¼ cup	50 mL
⅓ cup	75 mL
½ cup	125 mL
⅔ cup	150 mL
¾ cup	175 mL
1 cup	250 mL

TEMPERATURES

Fahrenheit	Celsius
32°F	0°C
212°F	100°C
250°F	121°C
275°F	140°C
300°F	150°C
325°F	160°C
350°F	180°C
375°F	190°C
400°F	200°C
425°F	220°C
450°F	230°C
475°F	240°C

COMMON COOKING & BAKING UTENSIL EQUIVALENTS

Bakeware	Imperial	Metric
Round Pan	8 × 1½ inches	20 × 4 cm
	9 × 1½ inches	22 × 4 cm
Square Pan	8 × 8 × 2 inches	22 × 22 × 5 cm
	9 × 9 × 2 inches	23 × 23 × 5 cm
Baking Dishes	11 × 7 × 1½ inches	28 × 18 × 4 cm
	12 × 7½ × 2 inches	30 × 19 × 5 cm
	13 × 9 × 2 inches	33 × 23 × 5 cm
Loaf Pan	8½ × 4½ × 2½ inches	22 × 11 × 6 cm
	9 × 5 × 3 inches	23 × 13 × 8 cm
Tube Pan	10 × 4 inches	25 × 10 cm
Jelly Roll Pan	15½ × 10½ × 1 inch	39 × 27 × 2.5 cm
Pie Plate	9 × 1¼ inches	23 × 3.2 cm
	10 × 1½ inches	25 × 4 cm
Muffin Cups	2½ × 1¼ inches	6 × 3.2 cm
	3 × 1½ inches	8 × 4 cm
Skillet	10 inches	25 cm
Casseroles and Saucepans	1 quart	1 L
	1½ quarts	1.5 L
	2 quarts	2 L
	2½ quarts	2.5 L
	3 quarts	3 L
	4 quarts	4 L

Note: The recipes in this cookbook have not been developed or tested in metric measures. When coverting to metric, some variations in recipe quality may be noted.

INDEX

General Mills, Inc.

Senior Editor: Jean E. Kozar

Recipe Development: Mary Hallin Johnson, Linel Reiber, Maureen P. Fischer

Nutrition Department Consultant: Nancy Holmes, R.D.

Recipe Copy Editor: Lauren Long

Editorial Assistant: Elaine Mitchell

Food Stylists: Mary Sethre, Cindy Lund, Catherine C. Condon

Photographer: Nanci Doonan Dixon

Photography Assistant: Scott L. Wyberg

Director, Betty Crocker Food and Publications Center: Marcia Copeland

Assistant Manager, Publications: Lois Tlusty

You will also enjoy these healthful cookbooks
from Betty Crocker:

BETTY CROCKER'S EAT AND LOSE WEIGHT

BETTY CROCKER'S LOW-FAT, LOW-CHOLESTEROL
COOKBOOK

BETTY CROCKER'S COOKBOOK